COUNSELLING CHILDREN

COUNSELLING CHILDREN

JEAN CAMPION

Whiting & Birch

LONDON
MCMXCI

Published by Whiting & Birch Ltd, PO Box 872, London SE23 3HL
London 1991

British Library Cataloguing in Publication Data
A CIP catalogue record is available from the British Library

ISBN 1 871177 10 3 (casebound)
ISBN 1 871177 07 3 (paperback)

Printed and bound in Great Britain
by Dotesios Printers Ltd, Trowbridge, Wiltshire.

CONTENTS

Acknowledgments

I should like to acknowledge a debt to Jill Crick and Judith Robertson, whom I knew as counsellors at Cranford Community School, Hounslow, during the 1980s. Between them they demonstrated just how effective counsellors can be in helping troubled and troublesome children.

I should also like to thank James Breese, Counsellor, British Psychological Society, for permission to use the case of "Pauline".

I am also grateful to Margaret Armitage who, over the years, has deciphered my handwriting and typed this and other manuscripts.

From time to time, I have used the expression(s) child psychology/ psychologist. There is actually no professional qualification of "child psychologist", but it is a useful means of referring concisely to both educational psychologists and those clinical psychologists who work with children.

I also refer to the school psychological service and child guidance clinics. These agencies, which exist to help children with developmental, behavioural and educational difficulties, may also be known as educational psychology services, or child and family centres, or other similar names.

INTRODUCTION

Children, in the nature of things, need the advice, support and encouragement of adults if they are to survive and grow and make the most of their particular circumstances. Parents normally provide this, but there are times when the help of other adults may be needed. This is particularly true when a child is under stress or living in difficult or unusual circumstances, or when he seems unable to respond to the normal challenges of everyday life at home or at school. On these occasions, access to an adult counsellor who is trained and experienced in working with children can make a great difference to a child.

But what exactly is counselling? The word is rather loosely used to describe a range of different activities, from those which might more properly be described as advice-giving (e.g. careers counselling) to those which have much in common with psychotherapy. The picture is further complicated by the fact that there are a number of different approaches and methods used by counsellors, which reflect their various philosophies, training and personal styles. Here, we are concerned with an activity which is described as personal or "client-centred" counselling. Based originally on the work of Carl Rogers, it is aimed at helping people to help themselves by encouraging them to think more clearly, and perhaps differently, about themselves and their circumstances; change or modify their behaviour or expectations; come to terms with situations which cannot be changed. It has a therapeutic component, but does not aim to explore or reveal deep-seated emotions or anxieties.

The methods used by all personal or client-centred counsellors are basically the same regardless of the age of the client, though modified to suit individual needs. Fundamental to the method is an ability and willingness to create a relaxed atmosphere in which communication can take place, and to listen attentively to what is being said. The counsellor needs to know how not to impose her own viewpoint on her client, while at the same time avoiding giving the impression that she agrees with all that is being said. Through experience, she learns that the client's view of a situation is not always the only possible view, and that there are rarely any straightforward solutions to the problems which people bring to their counsellors. She also knows that many of her clients need help to distinguish between those things in their lives which they might be able to change, and those which they cannot. Using her counselling skills to suit the needs of the case, she hopes that clients can be helped to gain some insight into their particular circumstances and predicament, modify their own behaviour and tackle their problems in a more realistic manner.

The counselling of children presents the counsellor with a particularly important challenge, and one which is rather different from that which arises from the counselling of adults. If the work is to be undertaken successfully, the counsellor needs - in addition to her basic counselling skills - a good knowledge of the state of childhood and of the ways in which children differ from adults. The differences are subtle, but important. The problems which children experience, and the ways in which they react to stressful situations are different. Unlike adults who from time to time complain about, and seek to change, certain things in their lives, children tend to take their personal circumstances for granted, and even to blame themselves when they find themselves in disagreeable situations which are not their fault, showing their stress and confusion indirectly through their behaviour. Thus, a child is much more likely to reach a counsellor because someone is worried by his unusual, troubled or troublesome behaviour, than because he has asked for help. There are exceptions to this - where, for example, a child approaches a sympathetic adult such as a familiar teacher with a request for help - but they are relatively rare.

Those who counsel children must also bear in mind that children are not independent beings but people who are emotionally attached to their parents and families, and dependent on parental care. Children have a right to an independent viewpoint, and in rare cases need to be protected from parental neglect or abuse, but they are not in a position to take responsibility for their own lives. Counsellors need always to remember this, and if there is occasion to feel concern about parental attitudes or behaviour towards a child, know how to act and whom to contact on behalf of the young client. They will also benefit if they can develop skills of parental interviewing, and knowledge of working with other adults who are involved with services to children (e.g. psychologists, social workers, teachers).

Counsellors must accept that children, though normally truthful and straightforward, do not always give an accurate picture of their circumstances and of how they are feeling, and that it is possible to have a false impression of how bad (or, indeed, how good) things are in the life of a particular child. One must also accept that many children are quite capable of manipulating a situation to their own, short-term, advantage, and of encouraging a sympathetic adult to take their part, whilst being less than open about their own misdemeanours.

In all circumstances, those who counsel children need to have their feet firmly on the ground and to know the limitations of their own efforts. Much can be done to help children whose lives are confused or unhappy but it is not possible to protect children from *all* suffering and anguish. As each child strives to achieve independence and personal competence alongside his peers, he or she must also be helped to come to terms with certain realities in life: that one cannot always have the things one wants, that the needs of other people must be considered and respected, that there are certain things which are inevitable and must be accepted.

Close personal contact with distressed and confused children over a period of time can create feelings of stress, anxiety and depression in the adult counsellor. It is emotionally demanding to listen to the problems of others, and particularly so when there quite often seems to be little that can be done to change the circumstances of a child's life. Ideally, the counsellor should have the regular support of someone else - a more experienced counsellor, perhaps - and access to a child psychologist or psychiatrist who can help and advise when needed. This also gives the counsellor an opportunity to consider the possibility of referring certain children to another agency when the problems seem too great for her to tackle alone. A counsellor also benefits - and will certainly work more efficiently - if she is not seeing clients all day and every day, but is combining her work as a counsellor with other work.

The scope of the book

There is at the present time a real and pressing need for trained counsellors who can address themselves to the problems which many children experience during the course of their daily lives. Fortunately, a number of people have seen the need and taken the trouble to develop the necessary skills which allow them to undertake the work successfully.

This book is written for them, to complement the training and the practice for which there is, of course, no substitute. It is assumed that readers have already acquired, or are in the process of acquiring, the skills of "client-centred" counselling and that they have regular contact with children. I would expect most of them to be working in the education system or with certain voluntary agencies, or in sections of the health and social services which are concerned with the welfare of children and their families.

In writing the book, I faced a dilemma when choosing cases to illustrate the counsellor's work. It seemed both inappropriate and unnecessarily sensational to focus on those highly stressful cases with serious implications which occasionally reach the headlines of the popular press, even though such cases do come the way of practising counsellors from time to time. On the other hand, it seemed equally as important to avoid giving the impression that counselling is no more than a "friendly chat", with children with minor difficulties. It was also difficult to choose between describing, say, two or three cases in detail, and offering a briefer description of a much larger number of cases. A choice of the first option would mean foregoing an opportunity to give an indication of the variety of different situations where counsellng skills are useful, and choosing the second risks giving the impression that counselling is a very superficial exercise.

Finally I decided to describe five children and their personal circumstances in varying degrees of detail, choosing cases which seemed to illustrate both the counsellor's skills and the type of problems with which she will probably be faced– although this will vary considerably according to the nature and purpose of the agency for which she is working. Since my own work has been mainly in a school psychological service and child guidance clinic, and my main contact with counsellors is through schools, there is an emphasis on problems which "surface" in schools. I make no apology for this. Some excellent counselling work takes place in schools, and a wide range of problems can be tackled. And counselling skills, once learnt, can be applied in a variety of situations to meet different needs.

Since children are dependent on their parents, and parents have certain responsibilities for their children, it seemed appropriate to pay some attention to the parental role and to the contact which a counsellor might have with the parents of a child she is trying to help. It also seemed necessary to consider the way in which counsellors might need to involve other people or other services from time to time, and to obtain help for herself - and the child - in more difficult cases.

But this is not a book about parents, nor about the network of services which exist to help children in need. Rather, it is an attempt to consider the counsellor-child relationship and the way in which the counsellor can make use of this relationship to help children with a wide variety of personal and social problems. Many of the problems are pressing and difficult to resolve. Nevertheless, in spite of this, many children can be, and are being, helped by their counsellors to develop greater confidence in themselves and in their abilities, along with a more realistic awareness of the needs and viewpoint of other people. From this solid foundation, they are better able to face the challenges and occasional tribulations of life with a good heart, and eventually to make the transition to competent adult status.

CHAPTER ONE

THE WORLD OF CHILDHOOD

The counsellor who works with children needs practical experience of their ways, and a working knowledge of their development and developmental needs. This should include a good understanding of the things that are likely to worry them, and of their methods of coping with personal difficulties and feelings of inadequacy. To some extent, this knowledge and understanding is a part of the shared experience of being human, and a result of the adult's own experience of childhood. On the other hand, childhood is very different from adulthood, and difficult - even impossible - to recapture with any degree of accuracy once it has passed. Counsellors who try to rely solely on their memories of personal experiences may well make errors of judgement when trying to help the children they see.

It goes without saying that those who counsel children need to like them - or, at the very least, to have a sympathetic understanding of the childish state. These feelings must, however, be founded on an acceptance of children as they are, rather than on the basis of a perception of childhood as it might be. A sentimental or idealised view is not helpful, since children are by no means always amiable victims. But nor are they as prone to misbehaviour as some would have us believe!

Each child, like each adult, has the potential for both good and bad behaviour, and each his* personal strengths and weaknesses. Like adults, they need to know how to tackle the challenges and occasional stresses of everyday living, and how to form steady relationships with other people.

---

*Counsellors and their clients may be male or female. However, I wish to avoid the excessive use of personal pronouns, and have decided to use "she" for the counsellor and "he" for the client unless the child under discussion is a girl. I hope that this arrangement is acceptable to the reader.

The counsellor's knowledge of childhood needs to include an understanding of children's social development, and an awareness of the feelings which children have for other members of their social groups. Family ties are particularly important. Children, particularly young children, are very attached to their parents, even when those parents do not seem, to the impartial observer, to be very good at meeting their needs. These feelings of affection are very strong in early childhood, though they change and sometimes weaken at a later stage. Most children are also very interested in their families and in family events and celebrations. Births, marriages, illnesses, changes in circumstances in the family circle, are all of interest to children. Inevitably, their views and opinions on these things will be coloured by the behaviour and the comments of the adults close to them.

During the pre-adolescent period, children are intensely loyal to their families, and counsellors hear much of "my mum/dad says...." from children between the ages of about 7 and 12. This tends to fade gradually during adolescence, as the peer group becomes more important and children begin to view their parents more critically. This is not, however, to suggest a waning of affection for the parents, but an increasing awareness in the child of his own feelings and point of view, and a natural inclination to move away from being his parents' child.

Self and other

Much has been written over the years about personal and social development. It is impossible to consider the subject in depth here, but important to remember that the feelings of confidence and self-esteem which help a child cope with the circumstances of his life and co-operate with other people begin to develop at a very young age. Initially pre-occupied with himself and his own needs, the young child gradually absorbs the rules of the social group and becomes aware of the needs and rights of other people. By the time he starts school -

indeed, well before this - he is, or should be, able to behave in a manner that is for the most part both sensible and acceptable to others.

Peer group relationships and the feelings of being accepted by others of the same age, are very important to children of school age. In junior school and the first year or two of secondary schooling, friendships tend to be with children of the same sex, and children of the opposite sex may be regarded with some embarrassment, or even hostility. (There are occasional exceptions to this.) Following the onset of adolescence, however, there is an increasing tendency for relationships with people of the opposite sex to be formed, though like-sex friendships are by no means abandoned. Indeed, they tend to strengthen and become more long-lasting.

Most children manage to become part of a social peer group, and to make and sustain friendships without too much difficulty. Some, however, experience considerable difficulty in this aspect of their lives. Counsellors know this, and are ready to help when necessary. They are aware that many children worry about their lack of friends and claim that other children are not very nice to them. However, they are also aware that children who do not have steady friendships with others often lack an ability to negotiate, share and tolerate the occasional differences of opinion which personal relationships always involve.

Counsellors are also aware that children usually find it easier to complain about the behaviour of other children than spend time thinking about themselves and their own behaviour. It is a good deal less painful to make a complaint about a playground incident than it is to discuss one's own attitude and the things which trouble one deeply. Knowing and understanding this, counsellors need to be able to develop their relationship with the children they see beyond the point where complaints are made and trivial incidents discussed, and towards a consideration of the child's circumstances and behaviour in a wider sense.

The vulnerability of childhood

Children, like the young of other species, cannot rear themselves and are dependent on adults for their protection, care, food, education, social and emotional well-being. This dependency is common to children of all societies, races and creeds, with certain relatively minor variations, particularly in the length of its duration. In the Western world, dependency usually lasts well beyond the biological state of childhood into adolescence or even early adult life, although there tends to be a period during which the young person is partly dependent on his parents and partly independent.

Children's dependence on the care and protection of adults is a fact of life which they themselves take for granted. They know that they need their parents, and hope to be loved and wanted in return. In most families, children receive at least an adequate amount of parental care and affection. Most also receive an appropriate amount of encouragement to obey the rules which adults make - rules which are designed partly for their own protection and partly for the protection of (or respect for) other people's well-being. Nevertheless, some children are less fortunate. Some are over-protected or indulged with worldly goods by parents who have little time for them. Others are expected to take considerable responsibility within the family, and to suppress their own personal needs or feelings to "fit in with" the requirements of others. A few are confused by conflicting adult messages, expected to behave in a responsible fashion at one moment, and to comply with unreasonable requests at another. A good example of this might be the child who is treated as an equal by a single parent, and then expected to efface himself when the parent takes on a new partner.

In some families, roles seem to be reversed and parents are very dependent on their children's practical or emotional support. The counsellor who works regularly with children becomes aware that a number of them tend to be burdened with a considerable amount of domestic responsibility, and responsibility for parental well-being. She will hear of 10-11 year old children taking younger siblings to school across busy roads or baby-sitting at night, and of children even younger helping sick mothers with shopping and cleaning. One ten year old described how she cooked breakfast for her younger brother and "burnt him" - a comment which raised considerable anxiety in the counsellor, eased somewhat by the knowledge that the brother was in school that day, and therefore presumably not badly hurt.

When deciding whether or not the home circumstances of a particular child need to be investigated, the counsellor will take several things into consideration. The child's age is obviously important, since younger children are that much more vulnerable and in need of protection than older children. Cultural factors may also need to be considered. In some communities, "latch key" children are so numerous that it seems inappropriate to worry about them, unless they are very young. And child-rearing practices do vary from one culture to another.

This is not an easy subject. Counsellors are aware that they must be tolerant of parental attitudes and sensitive to parental difficulties. Children must be prepared to co-operate with their parents and comply with their wishes for the most part. However, if a counsellor feels that a particular child is facing unreasonable hardship at home, or is being exploited or abused, she will want to take action. A referral to other agencies will probably be needed, and this is discussed in later chapters.

The importance of communication

Personal development and social cooperation depend very much on the ability and willingness of individuals to communicate with each other. Children learn much from what their parents tell them; they also need their parents to listen to them, answer their questions and help them think about things that are worrying them.

Families in which people communicate freely and where adults are able to give sensible and confident answers to their children are unlikely to disintegrate, and children who live in such families are fortunate. The experience of having a clear message of what is expected, and the opportunity to question and complain from time to time, will stand them in good stead as they grow older and form relationships with people outside the family circle. Children also benefit from the opportunity to see that people can disagree with each other, argue and then make good their differences by negotiation and compromise.

Although in most families parents communicate sensibly with their children and listen sympathetically to their children's efforts to communicate with them, in some families this does not seem to happen. Some parents do not seem to know what they expect of their children, or have expectations which are quite unreasonable. Messages to the children tend to be inappropriate and the children become confused and upset. At the same time, their efforts to communicate their feelings and experiences to their parents may be unsuccessful. No one is listening. Perhaps they do not even want to hear.

Parents are particularly unlikely to "want to hear" if the child is trying to communicate his anger at the parents' own behaviour. Adults who have acute difficulties in their own personal lives and marital/sexual relationships do not, on the whole, want to hear their children's expression of anger, sadness or despair as to what might be happening in the family. Nor do they find it easy to answer searching questions truthfully. Children can easily develop the feeling that they are wrong to be angry or to ask questions - rather than seeing that the weakness lies in the parent who cannot accept, or understand, or listen, or explain.

Counsellors realise that some of the children they see are having difficulty in communicating with their parents. They also understand that parents who are under stress themselves do not find it easy to listen to their children. In these cases, the counsellor's task is to prevent a total breakdown in communication between parents and children, and to bridge the gap in understanding that probably exists between them. Counselling sessions allow the child to express his feelings openly, if he wishes. At the same time, the counsellor has an opportunity, once she has developed a good relationship with her young client, to help him come to terms with difficult, or changing, domestic circumstances such as those which are associated with parental separation or divorce.

In a few families, there is a serious breakdown in communication, and children and parents drift farther and farther apart, sometimes with disastrous results. This occasionally happens when adolescent children find it impossible to adapt to the departure of one parent and the arrival of a step-parent. It can also happen when there are fundamental differences in attitude, expectations and opinion between a child's parents and the parents of his peers. This is a sensitive subject, particularly for children who live in families with cultural practices and standards of behaviour that are different from those of the indigenous population. Sometimes the tension between parental wishes and demands on the child and the child's experiences at school and with peers is intolerable and the gap impossible to bridge. However, counsellors can do much to help children reconcile differences in their lives and co-operate with their families whilst at the same time making and sustaining good relationships with friends from other cultural backgrounds.

Self-esteem

It is natural that children should seek to promote their own welfare - to stake a claim, as it were, on the world in which they find themselves and amongst the people who are important to them. The baby's insistent cry demands that he be noticed and fed. The toddler's challenge to parental rules demonstrates that he has a mind and will of his own. Older children argue with parents, and compete with siblings. These things are part and parcel of growing up and learning how to live in the social world. Children who can express their feelings and make a case for themselves stand a good chance of growing into sensible and competent adults. There is also a good chance that they will be able to respect the feelings of other people.

In their contact with others, children need to feel good about themselves. It is natural for them to protect their own self-esteem, even if this sometimes leads them to deny culpability or weakness. Very young children will say quickly "I'm not frightened" when they obviously are, or "I didn't do it" when they clearly have. If the adult response is sensible, children will grow out of this as they mature. With the passage of time, and increasing confidence, they learn that it is not so bad to admit to weakness, and that it is important to "own up" when at fault.

Some older children, particularly those who are socially immature and have low self-esteem, tend to respond like the very young child when under pressure. Confronted with adult anger, they deny what they have done and turn their attention to something or someone else. Other people are blamed, excuses are made, and a trivial incident becomes a source of frustration for an adult who is looking for a straightforward apology from the child. If a child only does this on rare occasions it may not be important, but for some children it becomes a way of life. Counsellors understand the temptation to deny responsibility and blame others, and allow for it when deciding what to believe and what not to believe. They know that it is unhelpful to put a child in a position from which he cannot retreat with his self-esteem reasonably intact. At the same time they hope to be able to encourage him to admit responsibility when he is at fault.

Facing up to reality

In their work with children counsellors know that they must aim to keep their young clients in touch with reality, and to avoid giving the impression that there are easy solutions to life's problems. For some children reality is tough, and counsellors must do their best to help them maintain self-esteem and personal equilibrium in extremely difficult circumstances. It may be a question of supporting and encouraging a child while there are serious family/domestic difficulties, or of helping him come to terms with his own disabilities, illness or personal and social problems while he gathers strength and increases in confidence. On the other hand, it is sometimes also a question of keeping a child in touch with the realities of the social world in which he lives. Many children find difficulty in understanding that their selfish or disruptive behaviour makes life disagreeable for other people; or fail to see that staying away from school, enjoyable in the short-term, damages their *own* long-term interests. Some must learn the hard way that anti-social behaviour brings its own retribution sooner or later.

There will always be a number of influences in a child's life which tend to distract him from social reality and the rights of other people. Counsellors may need considerable skill and persistence if they are to help children who are at risk of being led astray to develop the confidence and the competence they need to face up to - and enjoy - life as it is, rather than as one might ideally like it to be. But for the counsellor, too, reality is often tough. There are no easy solutions to the problems which some children experience, nor any easy way in which she can help them come to terms with this. In spite of this, the experienced counsellor knows that she can - and does - help many children who are caught up in traumatic events not of their own making or "stuck" in certain patterns of anti-social behaviour, outgrow their difficulties and move towards a more stable, acceptable, and satisfying way of life.

Children's rights

In this country (and perhaps in others) children's rights are defined in terms of the obligations which adults have towards them. This may seem a little unsatisfactory, but it is probably the most practical way to proceed. Children, particularly young children, are in no position to consider their "rights". Unlike adults, they are not expected to be fully responsible for their actions, and it is impossible to consider individual rights unless one also considers individual responsibility. Nor is it possible for a child to know what is best for him in the long run.

It is accepted that children need the care and protection of adults, and that preparations need to be made for their development and future. For example, the 1944 Education Act places a responsibility with local authorities to provide education for children in their area, and parents have a responsibility to ensure that their children attend school or at least that they receive an appropriate education. Children themselves do not have the right to choose whether or not they will attend school.

The principle of adult responsibility towards children is refined and extended in the recent Children Act (1989) . The concept of parental rights is diminished, and parents are expected to act in their children's best interests. At the same time, the local authorities are expected to take action when it is clear that parents are unable or unwilling to provide care and protection to their children, and they too are expected to put the welfare of the child first.

Although the Children Act does not focus attention on children's "rights", it requires that full attention be given to their wishes and feelings as well as their welfare (section 1 (3)(a)). It also seems that children may behave contrary to their parents wishes, provided that they stay within the law. That is to say, being beyond parental control is no longer, in itself, a reason for reception into Care. On the thorny subject of discipline, we are left with the conclusion that parents are expected to control their children in a reasonable manner. When deciding what is reasonable, as in deciding any other question under the Act, the Court would have regard to the child's age, sex and background, among other things (section 1 (3)(d)). So far, it is not illegal for parents to hit their children, as it is for teachers in the mainstream of education. On the subject of control, the Children Act recognises that some children may need to spend some time in secure accommodation (section 25).

Counsellors will be pleased to note that the Children Act places an obligation on local authorities to provide family centres where people can receive (among other things) counselling, and that children are given separate mention in connection with this (schedule 2, para 9(3)). Local authorities are also encouraged to facilitate others, including voluntary agencies, to provide services of this kind (section 17 (5)).

Those who are interested in learning more about the new legislation are referred to *Children: The New Law*, a very readable book by Andrew Bainham (Jordan and Sons, 1990).

CHAPTER TWO

STARTING WITH THE PROBLEM

An outsider's view of the work of a counsellor would probably be based on the notion that people ask for help when they have a particular problem in their relationships or working lives, or when they are living in distressing circumstances. This view is, however, much more accurate when applied to the counselling of adults, than it is to the counselling of children. With certain exceptions, which will be discussed in later chapters, children do not seek help for themselves, either because they are unaware that they have a "problem" which could be shared with other people, or because they do not know of the existence of a counselling service.

Most children reach a counsellor because an adult - usually, parent or teacher - is sufficiently worried by their behaviour or personal circumstances to seek help on their behalf. A child may, for example, be continually aggressive towards other children, or be staying away from school and indulging in anti-social or delinquent behaviour, or taking drugs. The actions which adults take on his behalf will depend much on what is available locally, as well as on the nature of the problem as the adults see it. Parents may seek the help and advice of the local school psychological services or child guidance clinic (these agencies are known by different names in different areas), or of certain voluntary agencies, and those services or agencies may provide a counsellor for the child. Teachers may refer children whose behaviour worries them to a school counsellor, if this facility is available in the school which the child attends, or to their local school psychological services. Doctors sometimes make a referral to an appropriate agency on a child's behalf, following a request for help by his parents.

Children reach counsellors in different ways and for different reasons, but it is always important that they know why they have been referred. This may seem obvious, but it is by no means certain that the irate or worried adult who has propelled a child in the counsellor's direction will have explained to him what he might expect. Sometimes, the referring adult has little understanding of the counsellor's role. She may also unwittingly give the child the impression that the counsellor is an authority figure who will scold or punish him.

Meeting a child for the first time, the experienced counsellor is aware of these things, and conscious that the child is probably anxious and uncertain as to what to expect from her. She knows that valuable time will be lost if this fear and uncertainty persists, and sets about putting the relationship on to a more realistic and helpful footing. She may ask the child if he knows why he has come to see her. If he seems uncertain or is silent, she gives a brief account of what others have told her about him, inviting him to comment if he wishes. Her manner is serious, but not unduly so, and she avoids putting any pressure on him to reply. Indeed, she may well decide against even asking him for his view of the matter, since she realises that she is unlikely to be told the truth, at least at this early stage in their relationship.

It may be hard for a counsellor, particularly if she is inexperienced, to accept the catalogue of misdeeds, which some quite innocent-looking children are supposed to have done, described by other adults. Occasionally, counsellors are faced with a child who denies vigorously that he was ever involved in the incident which has led to his referral, or lays the blame squarely on another child. She may even be inclined to believe him, if he looks innocent and indignant and makes a good case for himself.

Whatever the rights or wrongs might be over a particular incident involving a particular child, the counsellor works on the general principle that adults do not refer children to her without good cause. She is well aware that most of the children she sees need help to extricate themselves from difficult or damaging situations, which are quite frequently at least partly of their own making. True, in many cases other people will also be involved. However, this - for the time being at least - is not the concern of the counsellor.

Given that in most circumstances a child's behaviour will be damaging to himself or other people (or both), the counsellor will want to let him know that she disapproves of it. She will not labour the point, but will indicate to him that co-operation with other people rather than conflict is desirable, and that one should try and take the feelings of others into consideration in daily life. With an older child, she might speak briefly of the ill-effects of his behaviour in the long term, including possible exclusion from school and damage to his job prospects. If he is taking drugs or sniffing glue, she might comment in a concerned manner on the damaging effects of these substances.

This moral viewpoint is not, however, over-emphasised, since to do so would be unhelpful to the counselling relationship. The child has already had others telling him what he should or should not be doing, and the counsellor must take a different line as soon as possible. Having indicated briefly and quietly that she shares the same moral view as most other adults and that this is part of the reality of life, she moves on to other matters. Most important of all, she will need to get to know the child as soon as possible and to begin to help him think how he might change his ways, or his circumstances.

Getting to know the child.

Once the counsellor has established, briefly, her own point of view on the reasons for the child's referral to her, she will set about making a working relationship with him. She needs first to know something about his life, and about his interests, likes and dislikes, views of school and school work. She will probably ask him directly about these things, avoiding as far as possible the temptation to ask too many questions too quickly. From the beginning, she shows herself willing to listen to whatever is said, whether good or bad, without passing judgement or suggesting to the child what he should, or should not, say or think.

The counsellor also hopes to hear something about his family and family life. It may be easier to ask first about brothers and sisters, before moving to questions about his parents. Here, given the frequency of separation and divorce, the counsellor may experience certain difficulties. She needs to know the approximate structure of the child's family, and in particular which adults are caring for him on a daily basis, but she is also aware that such matters are very personal - and that the lives of some adults are very complex! She may perhaps ask the child whether both mum and dad live at home, or suggest that he tell her who is living in his house. The answer to these questions should give a clue as to what further questions may need to be asked.

It is worth commenting that those who counsel children are only interested in the lives of adults who care for them insofar as the adult behaviour might affect the child. It is helpful, for example, to know if both parents are in good health. Not infrequently, counsellors find that children are bearing a considerable burden at home because of the ill-health of a parent. If there has been a recent divorce or separation, it is helpful if a child can tell the counsellor if, and how often, he sees the absent parent, and whether there has been a replacement. Information which a child gives a counsellor on these or other subjects may not be strictly accurate, of course, but it is important. The counsellor keeps it in mind, whilst at the same time recognising that it may be necessary to gather further information perhaps from the parents themselves, at a later stage.

Listening to the child, the counsellor hopes to acquire a picture of his life and relationships with other people. This takes time, and is not necessarily easy to achieve. She also hopes to find some indication of the things that might be worrying him, or making him feel inadequate, guilty, and/or angry. Some children are quite open about their feelings, others are more circumspect. Some of the things about which some children express a strong opinion may not seem very important to an adult listener. Indeed, they may, in themselves, be quite mundane, while at the same time causing considerable stress to the child himself.

As she begins to get to know the child better, the counsellor will usually begin to understand some of the reasons for the difficulties which have prompted a referral to her for help. It may be that his troubled behaviour is related to a period of acute stress in his life, or to the confusing behaviour of adults close to him. It may also be that he has little understanding of what is, or is not, appropriate behaviour on his part. He is probably anxious and low in self-esteem, with few opportunities to feel good about himself. Little by little, and over a period time, the counsellor hopes to help the child feel more confident, think about himself and his circumstances, and change his attitudes and behaviour.

"Space" and the secure base

In her book, *Counselling Young People,* Ellen Noonan describes the nature of the counsellor's relationship with the client in the following terms:

> *A Counsellor has to establish a relationship which is firmly based in the reality of the everyday world, yet suspends reality enough so that the client can explore himself and take emotional risks in a way he has never before dared.*

Noonan's clients were young adults, not children, but her description of the counsellor's task fits well with the present discussion. Regardless of the age of the client, the counsellor is always seeking to provide him with the opportunity to communicate more freely and openly than he would normally. Her manner indicates the possibility of change, and of new ideas and new opportunities. At the same time, she has her feet firmly planted in reality, knowing that without the shared moral precepts of society both she and her client find themselves in very uncertain waters.

Noonan's counselling "model" is psychoanalytic, and the counsellor will not necessarily understand, or accept, all of psychoanalytic thinking. She can, however, learn much from the theories of certain child psychiatrists. The contributions of both Winnicott and Bowlby are particularly important, giving insight into the behaviour and the needs of children during the course of their development.

Two concepts are, I think, particularly useful to counsellors: Winnicott's concept of *space* and Bowlby's of the *secure base*. Both merit consideration here.

Winnicott uses the word *space* when discussing the parent-child relationship, to refer to the psychological distance between mother and child which defines their separate existence. He stresses the need for the parent to be able to respect and to understand the child's feelings as distinct from her own feelings. This may seem obvious, but it sometimes happens that parents identify so closely with their children that they fail to recognise that their child's point of view may well be quite different from their own.

This concept of *space* has many applications in child development. Broadly, it can be seen as a description of a child's need for the opportunity to develop his *own* thoughts and feelings through the experience of play, conversation, social contact and various activities suited to children. It assumes the willingness of adults to provide the opportunities, answer questions and set limits when necessary, offering encouragement, comfort and correction in an appropriate fashion.

Bowlby's ideas, though a little different, complement those of Winnicott. Basing his theories partly on the study of young animal behaviour and partly on psycho-analytic theory, Bowlby emphasises the importance of early social attachments. He stresses that the young child needs access to a stable adult figure, who provides him with a *secure base* from which he can make increasingly confident excursions into the surrounding environment, returning when he feels the need for comfort or reassurance.

Winnicott and Bowlby are concerned to describe the mother-child relationship during the early years of a child's life, and the counsellor may wonder what relevance this could have to her work with children. Clearly, it is inappropriate to make a *direct* comparison between the parental role and that of the counsellor. Nevertheless, counsellors - like parents - provide children with the *space* they need to develop their own thoughts, feelings and opinions. Like parents, they try to provide a *secure base* for children in the hope that they will use it to launch themselves, with increasing confidence, into the hurly-burly of daily life.

Active listening

Adults who have regular contact with children (for the most part parents and teachers) are unfortunately more likely to *talk* than listen to them. Children are told what to do, chastised, nagged, confided in, far more often than they are listened to. In a sense, this is a necessary fact of life, since adults have a responsibility to teach children the ways of the world and the social rules of the group in which they live. On the other hand, it can mean that a number of children have very little opportunity to give their own point of view and describe their own feelings and anxieties.

Counsellors know this and realise that it is very much part of their job to offer a willing and relatively neutral ear to their young clients. They listen carefully, hoping to be able to distinguish between those things that are important in the child's discourse and those which are not. They are aware that the children they see are, initially at least, anxious and afraid of criticism. It is important that they be encouraged, gently, to communicate.

It is not always easy for a counsellor to follow what a child is saying. Children who are anxious and low in self-esteem often talk in a confusing manner. If they are young, they also tend to assume that the listening adult knows more about them and the people and places which are familiar to them than she usually does. The counsellor may therefore find it difficult at times to follow the child's train of thought, or understand the detail of what he is trying to tell her. Sometimes it does not matter, but the counsellor may occasionally want to ask the child to clarify certain points. She will do this sparingly, however, and just often enough to be able to get a reasonably clear picture of what the child is trying to tell her.

The technique which the counsellor uses can be called *active listening,* or listening with a purpose. The counsellor knows why the child has been referred to her, and keeps this is mind as she talks and listens to him. She will be aware that the child's account of himself and his doings is designed to protect his self-esteem and deflect possible criticism. He may not be lying, but he is probably "playing down" his own misdemeanors and exaggerating those of other people. Her goal is that of helping the child to take responsibility for his own actions and to see the viewpoint of other people. At the same time, she continues to offer him support, encouragement and an attentive ear. The unspoken message is: "I like you and I want to help, but I cannot necessarily agree with everything you say".

From time to time, the counsellor may decide to modify what the child is saying, so as to put a more helpful slant on the situation and pave the way for change. It is as though she is saying, directly: "Well, yes, I believe you, but maybe you are exaggerating a bit. And maybe there is another side to the story, too". The case of Kevin, described below, demonstrates this.

THE CASE OF KEVIN (AGED 10)

Kevin has given intermittent cause for concern to his teachers throughout junior school. His relationship with other children is poor and he has been involved in several playground fights. In the classroom, his manner tends to be insolent and his school work below the level of that of his peers. Recently, his school attendance has begun to deteriorate.

Kevin's teachers find him troublesome, but they are aware that he is an intelligent boy who could do well. They are also conscious that he will soon be transferring to secondary school. Experience tells them that children who give cause for concern during the top year of junior school have great difficulty in adjusting to the more formal requirements of secondary schooling. Kevin is referred to a school counsellor, with his mother's permission.

Early in the first session, the counsellor lets Kevin know that she is aware that he has been in trouble quite frequently. She decides that she will not mention, for the time being, the playground fights and the insolence to teachers. Quietly, she asks him why he stays away from school. He shrugs and does not answer. After a brief silence, the counsellor asks him if he likes school. Kevin shrugs again. After another brief silence he tells her that it is "not bad".

The counsellor then says a little about getting into trouble. Does he realise that his teachers are worried about this? Kevin fidgets in his chair. He is a small boy, rather untidily dressed and with very short hair. After a while he says:

"There's this kid. He's always beating me up".

The counsellor nods, but says nothing.

Kevin continues: "I wasn't doing nothing to him! He kicked my bag. And pushed me over. Then the teacher said it was my fault!" His voice is indignant. "He's always doing it!"

After a short pause, the counsellor says: "Mmmm. I see. It sounds rather difficult...."

Kevin says: "They're always picking on me".

It is unclear as to whether Kevin is referring to the other boy, or to the teachers. However, there is a general feeling of unhappiness, and the counsellor decides that she needs to show understanding while at the same time calming the situation. She says: "So....there's often trouble between you and this boy."

"His name is Darren". Kevin tells her.

"I see. Have you known him for long?"

Kevin shrugs. "I don't remember...."

"I was wondering ... it might be rather difficult ... but, could you perhaps try keeping out of his way."

Kevin looks doubtful. "He's always picking on me...."

"Well, yes, I can see that it is a difficult situation. But maybe you could give it a try for a few day?"

Having said this, the counsellor knows that she must now move on to other things. There is no useful advantage to be gained by continuing with this part of the discussion at this point. Nevertheless, the foundation for the counselling relationship has been laid. The counsellor has indicated that she hears the child and is not directly contradicting his point of view, nor arguing with him. At the same time, she has taken the heat out of the situation, by avoiding the use of aggressive words such as "beating up" or "picking on". She has also hinted that the child himself might have contributed to the problem ("So there's often trouble *between* you"), and indicated that it might at some stage be possible for the child to change his own behaviour.

Having made these points and planted the notion of change and improvement in the child's mind, the counsellor moves to other topics. Kevin responds to her suggestion that he tell her about his favourite subjects at school. He likes metalwork and art, he says. This leads the counsellor to ask about his Dad. Is he good with his hands? Before long Kevin is talking about fishing expeditions with his father and about the garden shed he helped his father build. Later, the counsellor will hear about his mother, whose long-standing ill-health has resulted in recent hospitalisation and, inevitably, in disruption to the family routine. Sadly, the fishing expeditions no longer take place, as Kevin's father struggles to keep his job while looking after the family.

During this first session, several important things have happened. Kevin has discovered that the counsellor will listen to him, and is prepared to try and understand his point of view. The counsellor, for her part, is beginning to know Kevin. She was originally aware that his relationship with other children is poor and that he can behave badly. In addition to this, she now understands that he is an anxious child, and worried about family matters. She will want to consider the possibility of discussing the situation at school with Kevin's teachers, and perhaps intervening in what seems to be a certain amount of playground misbehaviour and even bullying. (See later section). She will also want to consider the possibility of meeting Kevin's parents. After some thought, she decides to postpone taking either of these steps for the time being. She invites Kevin to return the following week.

At the next session, Kevin arrives early. He is relaxed and talkative, and tells the counsellor that he is an uncle. This takes the counsellor by surprise, as she had not realised that Kevin had older brothers or sisters. She questions him gently, and learns that his father has been married before. Kevin has two half-sisters and one of them has recently given birth to a boy, whom Kevin has just met. This is interesting news. There is no time to discuss with Kevin his relationship with other children at school. She listens while he describes the baby, and learns a little more abut the family.

Before seeing Kevin the following week, the counsellor decides that it is necessary to ask his teachers about his attendance and his behaviour. He has been absent only twice in the two weeks since the counselling started, and there have been no major incidents in either the classroom or the playground. At the counselling session, the counsellor asks Kevin directly how he has been getting on recently at school. Is there anything that he would like to tell her? Kevin shrugs. There does not appear to be anything worrying him greatly, and the counsellor does not press him on the matter. However, just before the session comes to an end, Kevin tells the counsellor, rather sadly, that no-one seems to like him very much. It is too late to discuss it, but she nods sympathetically and arranges to see him a few days later.

During the fourth session, Kevin begins to reveal rather more of himself, and a picture of a child who is quite seriously lacking in self-esteem emerges. Other people "don't like" him, and he is "no good" at his school work. He "never seems to have any luck", he says sadly.

The counsellor lets him talk for a while, and listens sympathetically. She decides to tell him that his teachers know that he is quite a clever boy, even if his work is not always as good as it should be. He is surprised - and obviously pleased - that anyone should think him clever. *He* thinks he is stupid. Maybe, then, he could describe some of the things that he finds difficult to understand, and ask a few questions?

This is not easy for Kevin, but with the counsellor's encouragement he begins to talk about some homework, which he has been set, which he does not understand very well. They spend some time on this, and the counsellor then suggests he ask his teacher next time he doesn't understand something. At the next session, he reports that he has done this, with success.....

Little by little, the counsellor aims to increase Kevin's self-esteem while at the same time trying to encourage him to make a greater effort on his own behalf. She knows that once his confidence begins to increase, he will not only feel better about himself but will behave more acceptably. Better results in the classroom and more favourable responses from teachers will have a cumulative effect, and Kevin will go from strength to strength.

The counsellor also knows that there are a number of children like Kevin, who are both victims and aggressors at school. Without help, they tend to go from bad to worse, becoming increasingly alienated and perhaps out of control. However, with the help and encouragement which the counsellor tries to offer, they can learn to think constructively about themselves and their behaviour, and begin to change.

CHAPTER THREE

COMMUNICATION AND CHANGE

The counsellor starts with the assumption - indeed, the confident expectation - that people have within themselves the potential for change, and a desire to improve their circumstances, including their own behaviour. She knows that her clients want to be able to lead their lives competently and make good and lasting relationships with other people, even though the things they do often seem unhelpful, annoying, immature, incomprehensible, destructive. Training, and the experience of real improvement in many or even most of her clients, encourage her to believe that with rare exceptions there is no good reason why someone should remain forever "stuck" in a situation which cannot be improved, or destined to repeat patterns of behaviour which make life intolerable for himself or for others.

Working with children the counsellor often takes on considerable responsibilities, but she has the advantage of working with a young and flexible creature. There is a real opportunity in most cases to set in motion a process of change, so that a child moves away from negative and damaging patterns of behaviour, towards more co-operative and constructive ways of living. At the same time, the counsellor does not underestimate the powerful "pull" of the old ways and the human tendency to resist change even when recognising the need for it. Nor does she overlook the possibility that there are damaging influences in a child's life, outside his control, which are interfering with his well-being and good development.

Counsellors realise that most of their young clients are suffering from feelings of inadequacy, conflict, anxiety, guilt, confusion, despair - although they will not necessarily admit to them. These negative feelings get in the way, and prevent the child from making the most of his opportunities, and from concentrating on his school work or making friendly and relaxed contacts with other people. Many of these negative and unhelpful feelings are related to a child's personal circumstances, and counsellors know that children benefit from talking about their experiences and the things that trouble them. This opportunity encourages them to develop an awareness that these feelings need not overwhelm them. It can also help them to understand the difference between those things which *are* their responsibility (e.g. their behaviour at school) and those which are not, such as their parents' domestic and social difficulties.

But children do not always find it easy to put their thoughts and feelings into words and to talk freely and honestly to an adult, however sympathetic that adult might be. Indeed, it is worth thinking about this reluctance from the child's point of view. Adults are powerful creatures who lead lives that are largely unknown to children. Sometimes they are irritable, remote, evasive, angry for reasons which the child does not understand. Occasionally they laugh about something which does not seem funny to the child. They ask questions, but children learn that an honest reply is not expected from them. Few adults who bother to ask expect a child to say that he *didn't* enjoy a party or an outing, *doesn't* like his baby brother, feels fed up, angry, upset, confused. Almost invariably, children are expected to reply in a way that does not stir the adult conscience, or upset the adult's view of things. Yes, the party was nice, the new baby lovely. No, he didn't hurt himself/ "mind" when people changed their plans....

Counsellors, on the other hand, want their young clients to be truthful. When they ask a question, they do not want a polite reply, but one which reflects the child's real feelings: difficult, indeed, for many children to understand. It gets easier with time, however, and children who develop trust and confidence in their counsellors find that there is real relief in being honest and open. Indeed, it is the counsellor's ability both to (gently) encourage children to make this emotional commitment, and to accept what is said to them by the child, that lies at the heart of good counselling.

Giving time

How much time should a counsellor expect to offer her young clients? This varies from case to case, and depends as much on the particular responsibility which the counsellor has for the client as it does on the child's problems. If the counsellor is easily available to the child (as for example she might be if she works in a large comprehensive school), it might be helpful - and possible - for the child to be seen for a brief session daily, for a limited period of time, perhaps while he is going through a difficult period. On the other hand, if the child has to visit the counsellor some distance away, losing time from school lessons as he does so, a longer session, less frequently held, is a more realistic proposition.

Since children are, by virtue of their youth, less "stuck" in their ways and more amenable to change than adults, much can be done in five or six weekly sessions, particularly if the work is complemented by additional work with the adults close to the child (usually, parents and teachers). Sometimes, more time is needed, although the counsellor needs to be wary of continuing to see a particular child over a long period of time, without occasionally considering her position and perhaps discussing her client with a colleague. This is particularly important if a child's behaviour or circumstances are not changing, or if the counsellor feels she is not getting to know him any better. Cases which "drag on", unresolved, usually need to be referred to other agencies who have different powers, or resources, at their disposal and can therefore adopt a different method of helping a child.

The tip of the iceberg

Children are usually referred to counsellors because something they have done upsets, annoys or worries adults, and counsellors bear this in mind when they see a child. However, counsellors also realise that the troubled or troublesome behaviour is almost invariably the visible "tip of the iceberg". Behind the behaviour (or below the surface) lie many troubled and confused feelings and unhappy experiences with which the child needs help.

It is not always easy for a child to communicate his feelings and describe his experiences, and counsellors need to be alert to the various possibilities. As we have seen in the case of Kevin in the preceding chapter, some children provide information which gives the counsellor the opportunity to learn about matters which are worrying the child. On the other hand, it can be extremely helpful if an adult close to the child is willing and able to impart personal information which helps the counsellor to understand a child's predicament. In the case described below, Jenny's father volunteered the information that he and his wife had recently been through a very painful divorce. This was helpful to the counsellor, who describes the case, below.

THE CASE OF JENNY

Jenny was brought to my notice while she was still at junior school by her father who was asking for help since she had been caught stealing from a local shop. Jenny was just 11, and she and her sister (who was13) were being brought up by their father following their parents' divorce. Jenny's father was also worried because he was aware that she was stealing from him as well.

Jenny was due to transfer to secondary school in a few months' time. I saw her twice before she started in the secondary school and established a relationship with her. The relationship, which proved helpful to her, continued during the first year of secondary schooling. It was clear that Jenny missed her mother very much, and she spoke mainly about her sad feelings at losing her. Before long, the stealing from shops and from the father stopped.

Jenny's father was considerably upset by the breakdown of his marriage, and seemed to find it difficult to accept that the children wanted - and needed - to continue to see their mother. I managed to persuade him to consider the possibility of establishing regular visits to the mother, and he eventually agreed. He was a quiet, shy man who seemed able to understand the link between Jenny's stealing and her feelings of loss.

It is interesting to note that Jenny's stealing stopped quite soon after she had begun to talk about her mother and the break up of the family to the counsellor. Though the sessions continued, the most important part of the task seemed to be completed quite quickly. No doubt it would have been helpful if Jenny could have expressed her feelings to her father at the time of the divorce. Perhaps she sensed his deep distress, and felt unable to burden him further with unhappy feelings of her own. This situation is very familiar to those who counsel children. Time and again they find themselves listening to children who, for one reason or another, are not able to share their feelings with their parents.

Promoting change in behaviour

Children whose anti-social or troubled behaviour is associated with stressful events in their lives usually begin to improve once they have the opportunity to talk about the things that are troubling them. Nevertheless, the improvement is not necessarily immediate. In Jenny's case, the stealing stopped quite quickly. In the case of Kevin in the preceding chapter, however, the counsellor needed to combine sympathetic listening with suggestions that a change of attitude and behaviour was needed. Each case is different and merits a slightly different approach from the counsellor. Much of the skill lies in balancing sympathy with the right degree of firmness.

When working with unhappy, anxious or confused children who are behaving in an anti-social manner, the counsellor needs to be aware of the danger of giving a child the impression that his unhappy circumstances excuse his bad behaviour. "You are stealing/behaving aggressively because you are un-happy" is *not* a helpful message for any child to receive, even indirectly, from an adult. Rather, the counsellor hopes to con-vey to the child "I hear what you say and sympathise with your difficulties. Things *can* improve. Now, let's see what can be done" . This message is flexible and encouraging. At the same time, it does not dismiss the problem as trivial, or the child's feelings as unimportant.

Offering a mixture of sympathy and firmness , the counsellor helps the child to reconsider his own behaviour, and to understand the viewpoint and feelings of other people. Counsellors learn with experience just how much pressure can be put on any child to consider changing his own behaviour, and when to do this. Some children find it very difficult to move from a point of blaming other people for everything to one where they can consider their own behaviour and attitudes, whilst other do not.

As she begins to know a child, the counsellor may make the occasional practical suggestion as to how he might help him-self. The idea of keeping out of the way of those who cause trouble can be a useful beginning. Simple techniques such as counting to ten before responding to teasing or provocation may also be suggested, with good results. Some children re-spond well to the suggestion that they behave "sensibly" - an expression which seems less challenging than "being good". Having made a practical suggestion to a child as to how he might conduct himself on future occasions, the counsellor needs to check with him at the following meeting as to how he "got on", or "managed". Success (e.g. at keeping out of trouble for a few days) should be praised, and further encouragement given.

Children who have been troublesome for a long period of time often, unfortunately, have a bad reputation to overcome, and tend to be blamed for situations which are not their fault as well as for those which are. Adults who know the child tend to behave towards the child in a very negative manner, and it is extremely difficult for him to be accepted as an ordinary member of the community. There really is no easy answer to this. The child needs to be encouraged to see that with the passage of time his past reputation will fade, and in the meantime he must make an extra effort to behave sensibly, with the counsellor's help and encouragement.

Should one investigate?

Counsellors almost invariably hear complaints from the children they see about the behaviour of others. Some of the complaints may well be justified, but the child who talks about being bullied or "beaten up" is quite often exaggerating. Again, this is a difficult subject and each case is different, but counsellors learn not to take action at the first indication that their young client is a victim. Experience tells them that the child is probably withholding information about his own tendency to taunt other children, stir up trouble, behave annoyingly.

Children with low self-esteem have a depressing tendency to find themselves in situations which more confident children avoid. As we have seen, counsellors can help considerably in this, by offering a mixture of sympathy and friendly advice. However, it is occasionally necessary to investigate a child's complaints against others. A meeting between the adults who know the child can be helpful; so, too, is a period of time spent quietly observing the child with others in the playground (where so many incidents are said to occur). Interventions which include identification and punishment of wrong-doers should only be undertaken rarely and in extreme cases. All-too-often it is possible to make matters worse and, hard though it may seem, the child who is a victim usually benefits more if he can change *his* behaviour than if adults intervene to punish his peers. If the bullying and fighting are extreme, however, the matter needs to be tackled with the school as a whole, by senior members of staff.

When a child complains of the behaviour of others *at home*, the counsellor needs to be particularly cautious. In the first place, she cannot be sure whether he is really as "put upon" as he says that he is. Equally as important, she will not want to undermine parental authority unless there is a very good reason for doing so. However, the counsellor will take the child's age into consideration, as well as the things of which he complains, when she decides how to tackle this delicate matter. Older children can be encouraged to see the parental point of view and make allowances for it, while at the same time developing personal strengths and interests outside the family. Younger children, however, may be suffering quite serious neglect, hardship or even abuse at an age when they are still highly dependent on parental care. In cases of this nature, the counsellor will need to seek advice (Chapter Eleven).

The silent child

Although most children respond quite well to their counsellors, perhaps after an initial period of uncertainty, the occasional child remains completely silent and apparently unmoved. This is a frustrating situation, and the counsellor is left with feelings of anxiety about the child and about what he might be hiding, and of inadequacy at her inability to encourage him to talk.

It is tempting, when faced with a mute, perhaps rebellious, child to take the initiative and talk oneself, particularly if one knows a child has behaved wrongly or dangerously. However, an adult who talks at length to - or at - a child about his unruly behaviour or the unfortunate consequences of, say, drug-taking is unlikely to bring about change in the child's behaviour. Faced with a barrage of adult words, however relevant and well-meant, the child is likely to retreat still further behind the wall of rebellious silence - and to return to his previous behaviour after the session.

In some cases, the counsellor will be aware that a child is keeping silent to protect other people. It may be that he fears retribution from his peers if the counsellor tells others that he is being victimised. Even more serious a situation arises when the counsellor suspects that a child's silence hides an unhappy secret within his own family. Children whose parents abuse them may be fearful of communicating their distress to other people. Indeed, they may well have been told by their parents that "telling" would lead to a break up of the family, and their own reception into Care.

If the counsellor's efforts to encourage conversation fail, she may usefully indicate to the child that she recognises that it is hard for him to talk for the present time. She will try to ensure that he knows where to find her should he change his mind, and will suggest that she would be pleased to see him if he cares to call one day. If it seems appropriate in the light of the information she has been given about the child, she may indicate to him that she recognises that his silence might be due to a desire to protect other people.

It is always helpful to remember that children can gain something from what feels, from the counsellor's point of view, like a sterile and useless meeting. Next time, it might be possible to communicate - perhaps to someone else, if not to the counsellor herself.

CHAPTER FOUR

CHANGE AND CHANGING CIRCUMSTANCES

Children are flexible creatures, and most of them are well able to adapt to new circumstances and to changes in their lives, including a change in caregivers. The instinct to survive and develop is strong, and most children can, and do, come to terms with new situations quite quickly, and adapt to new people without too much difficulty. This is not to suggest that they do not experience anxiety, sadness or anger when the stable pattern of their lives is disrupted. These feelings are particularly intense when there is disruption in family life, and a parent is lost through divorce or (less commonly) death. Indeed, the feelings of loss and confusion can sometimes persist over quite a long period of time, preventing a child from functioning as he should.

Change in family circumstances may mean the arrival of a new parent-figure, and this can also create difficulties for children. The existence of a stepfather brings home to a child the reality of his parents' divorce, when he might secretly have hoped for a reconciliation. He must also get used to this new person, who has his own ways of doing things, likes and dislikes, methods of discipline. Sometimes, the new father-figure is very young, so that the relationship is rather more like an uncertain peer-relationship, than one between parent and child. At the same time, the child may worry about the absent parent, particularly if he/she is living alone.

There are probably other changes, too, for the child whose parents decide to part company: a change of house and school, step-brothers or sisters, new aunts, uncles and grandparent figures. There may also be subtle changes, hard to evaluate.

For example, a child who lives for a long time alone with one parent following a divorce tends to become very close to the remaining parent. He/she may be allowed to stay up late at night as "company" for the parent, or even to share the parental bed. An older child may be expected to take on an adult, or near-adult, role, perhaps taking responsibility for the younger children or becoming a "confidante" as the sole parent learns to live alone. This may work quite well for a while - though it sometimes leads to children missing school - but there may be serious difficulties if the parent finds a new partner. With the advent of a new parent-figure, the child is demoted from adult status, and becomes a child again. It may come as a welcome relief, but it more often seems to cause feelings of dispossession and jealousy. It can also lead to arguments, even violence in the family, at least for a considerable period of time as all of the members of the family adjust to the new situation.

Children are more likely to adapt to changes in their lives in a flexible and positive fashion if they have the opportunity to express a point of view, and to have their questions answered sensibly. Too often, parents seem to take for granted their children's acquiescence, and fail to see that the change of circumstances which is a pleasure for *them* may be a source of distress for a child. For one reason or another, many parents fail to talk sensibly to their children about their decisions, to respect their wishes to see the absent parent, to understand the difficulties the children may have in accepting a new parent-figure.

Counsellors see many children who are upset by changes in their family circumstances. Indeed, their sympathetic ear, linked with an awareness of the need to help the child, little by little, to understand the parental point of view, helps many children to come to terms with circumstances beyond their control. The same children can also be helped, over a period of time, to understand that what has happened in their families is not *their* fault, and that parental happiness is not *their* responsibility. This understanding should bring with it a welcome awareness in the child that he has his own life to lead and to enjoy.

Transition

Some of the changes which take places in the lives of children are, or should be, basically pleasurable even if they are associated with some degree of anxiety. The transition from infant to junior school, and from junior to secondary school are good examples of changes that are on the whole welcomed by children as a sign of "growing up", even though they may also be associated with some uncertainty and apprehension. As far as counsellors are concerned, they are unlikely to see many infant/junior school transition children but will almost certainly see a number of children in the first year of secondary school who are having difficulty in adjusting to the new routine.

Most adults can probably remember their own feelings about transfer from junior school to a large secondary school. The change is full of challenge and excitement for children although it also tends to be fraught with a considerable amount of anxiety for many of them. Junior schools tend to be small, friendly places where everyone knows everyone else, and where the Head knows and understands each child. There is discipline, of course, but allowance is usually made for certain children, and tolerance shown for occasional misdemeanours and mistakes. Children know all of the members of staff, and have come to predict their behaviour and to adapt themselves to it.

This state of affairs changes when a child enters secondary school. Here, he is immediately confronted by a large building and a number of unfamiliar adult faces. He is supposed to organise himself, know the rules and accept the occasional angry word from a teacher when he, often inadvertently, transgresses. Most children adapt to the change quite quickly but for some it is extremely difficult. They lose books, pens and sports equipment, cannot remember or fail to find the classroom where they are supposed to be, do not know what home work they have been set. If they are reprimanded, they may unfortunately answer cheekily, or angrily, or become even more confused and upset. In some cases, school attendance is so painful, that children begin to stay away with imaginary aches or pains.

Experienced teachers are aware that the transfer to secondary school is stressful for less socially confident children, and most will make a deliberate effort to ease the transition from one school to another. During the last term or so of junior school, attempts are usually made to prepare the children for the change. A visit to the secondary school may be arranged, while secondary school teachers arrange to visit "feeder" junior schools to meet their future pupils. Discussions take place, and the children who are due to transfer are encouraged to ask questions about their future school.

Once the children have changed school, the teachers in the first year of secondary school may go to considerable lengths to help the children settle into the routine of the school day, and to understand what is required of them. Teachers, whose responsibility it is to help the new intake of pupils, benefit if they have some knowledge of counselling techniques. And, of course, the whole school as well as individual children will benefit if there is an experienced counsellor on the staff.

In spite of the best efforts of teachers to help children to make a good start in secondary school, some first year children fail to adapt. Such a child was Lee, and his case is described below.

THE CASE OF LEE

Lee arrived at his secondary school from another part of the country, and had not therefore benefited from an opportunity to visit the school or to meet any of the teachers. Perhaps even more important, he knew none of the children. Junior school records which accompanied him made reference to attention-seeking behaviour, but his school work was reasonably good. He was 11½ a good looking boy, small for his age and bright-eyed with, it seemed, enthusiasm.

In spite of his considerable personal strengths, he was soon in trouble. He seemed unable to learn where he should be at different times of the day, looking blank when reminded, or corrected. Homework, pencils and P.E. kit were continually missing, and Lee seemed to have no idea of where his things might be. When chastised, he smiled but showed no signs of improving. Staff liked him personally, but found him annoying, and worrying. Finally, a member of staff who took it upon herself to counsel certain pupils - and who had followed a course in counselling - decided to see Lee on a regular basis.

In his sessions with the counsellor, Lee was friendly, chatty, yet quite difficult to know. He had come from the north of England to the London area, and he told the counsellor about his school and his friends whom he had left behind. He spoke too of his family, describing activities and outings, and the games which he played with his brothers and sister. It all seemed quite normal, and the counsellor found herself wondering why Lee showed little sign of settling down. Admittedly he had had the disadvantage of arriving in a new area and starting at a new school at the same time. But with the passage of time, and the counsellor's help, he should have settled into the new routine. Yet he showed no sign of doing so.

After three sessions, the counsellor decided she would try to be a little more challenging. She looked rather sternly at him and said, quietly: "Other children seem to do as their teachers ask, Lee. Why are you always doing the wrong thing?"

Lee was silent. He seemed unmoved, but was for once lost for words.

Counsellor: "Why, Lee? There must be a reason".

Lee : "I don't know" . His face was blank.

Counsellor: "Is it quite impossible for you to remember your books and be in the right place at the right times?"

Lee: "Don't know....."

There was a pause, while they looked at each other.

Counsellor: "Maybe I should try and see your mum and dad".

Lee looked rather awkward: "My dad works".

Counsellor: "I'm sure he does. But maybe he has some time off. And what about Mum?"

Lee was silent, and the counsellor began to feel rather uneasy. On the face of it, the conversation was straightforward. Yet something seemed wrong. Some further investigations were needed. She wrote to Lee's parents and invited them to come into school.

During the time he had been seeing Lee, the counsellor had formed an impression of his parents from the description Lee gave of the family. They sounded quite young and lively, and she was quite unprepared for the large woman in her forties who arrived at the meeting alone. She sat heavily in the chair and began to tell the counsellor details of life since Lee's father had left when he was a baby. The story was rather incoherent, but it appeared that they had moved house several times, and that she had recently formed a liaison with a much younger man. There were three young children, two boys and a girl, from this relationship.

The counsellor was pleased that the mother had come to see her, and told her so. Nevertheless, she was somewhat frustrated by the interview. The mother's account of Lee's past life and experiences was not very coherent, and the counsellor felt unable to pose too many direct questions. It was, however, clear that the mother thought highly of Lee, and was unable to understand why his teachers were concerned about his behaviour. She described him as "helpful" at home, and insisted that he was "no trouble". When the meeting was over, the counsellor was left with the impression that Lee's behaviour at school was all the fault of his teachers, and that he himself was without fault. Yet she was well aware that this was not so.

In spite of its apparently unsatisfactory nature, the meeting seemed to help. Although he did not say so openly, Lee seemed to be encouraged by his mother's meeting with the counsellor. He began to talk more freely about his family, and the counsellor heard details of Lee's home life of which she had previously been unaware. Lee began to complain about the noisy younger children at home, the lack of space, shortage of money and the endless chores with which he was expected to help. He spoke, too, of the frequent changes of school, and of the friendships which had been made, only to be broken as the family moved house yet again. Most important of all, the counsellor heard of the man with whom Lee's mother lived for a while, before forming her current (and relatively stable) relationship, who used to beat him.

Life had been - was - tough for Lee, despite his chirpy manner. For a while, the counsellor considered the advisability of involving the local social services department. However, it seemed that the worst of Lee's problems were actually in the past, and that he was not currently at risk. The counsellor felt that, with encouragement, Lee could begin to put the past behind him, and learn to become more confident and well-organised, and less attention-seeking. Her confidence in Lee proved to be justified. As he became aware that it was possible to share his more unhappy experiences with the counsellor, Lee also became more willing to accept advice and correction about his behaviour.

Lee's case is an example of the need for the counsellor to think flexibly, and to be prepared to change her approach. The early counselling sessions were full of inconsequential chatter, and an inexperienced counsellor might well have thought that there was nothing wrong, nothing which needed to be shared and discussed. A change of tactics and a slightly sterner approach silenced Lee, and made the counsellor realise that it was worth making further investigations. The subsequent meeting with the mother provided the counsellor with some slight but significant insight. More important, it gave Lee the confidence he needed to become more open and honest with the counsellor, to his own advantage.

The changing child

Children are constantly and rapidly changing, and adults need to be able to take account of this in their dealings with them. The rules which parents make for their children need to be changed as they grow older; so, too, do parental expectations. It may seem obvious, but it is worth remembering that some parents have difficulty in taking account of the passage of time, in matters concerning their own offspring. For example, some may fail to see that the protective attitudes which they have adopted with their 8 or 9 year old children need to change once the children start in secondary school, or understand the adolescent need for some personal privacy and independence.

It is not, of course, possible to be precise as to what rules are appropriate at any given age, and when they need to change. But it is necessary to bear in mind that children need to be guided towards taking greater responsibility for themselves and their own actions, as they grow older. There is often work to be done here, for the counsellor. A number of children whom she will see will come to her notice because they are behaving in a way that might have been appropriate when they were much younger, but no longer is. Such children need help to "grow up" a little. At the same time, the counsellor may find it helpful to meet with parents, and discuss with them the rules and the expectations which prevail in the family. (Interviews with parents are considered in Chapter Ten).

The adolescent change

Counsellors will almost certainly see a number of children who are on the verge on adolescence, and they therefore need to be aware of the particular problems associated with this age group. Many children, previously quite docile, begin to behave badly when they reach the age of about 13. Some also experience considerable difficulties in their relationships with their parents, whilst a few take the drastic step of running away from home. The reasons for the children's problems vary, but a common factor is the drive towards independence and the way in which this sometimes conflicts with the child's need for adult direction and control. All too often, children at this important stage in their lives find themselves left very much to their own devices, when they need their parents to show interest in them *and* to set certain limits on their behaviour.

The onset of adolescence is a difficult time for children of all social backgrounds, but it is a particularly stressful time for those who feel that the future does not hold, for them, very many opportunities. Such children may also feel that their teachers' expectations are too high. School leaving examinations appear on the horizon and there is a change of pace in the classroom. The work is harder and the amount of homework increases, and a number of children begin to realise that the gap between them and the cleverer children is increasing all the time. Despair sets in and they drift away from school. Once out of school for long periods of time, it becomes increasingly difficult for them to follow the curriculum. Even more worrying, such children are at risk of being caught up in delinquent or damaging behaviour during the time they are not at school.

Teachers are of course aware of the problem, and most local authorities have a policy for educating less able children which encourages them to remain at school, at least until the statutory school-leaving age. Many also have good work-experience programmes for children. Local authorities also provide certain opportunities for vulnerable children (e.g.

intermediate treatment schemes for delinquent, or potentially delinquent, children).

Children of this age-group need a lot of support, and many of them are in need of the help of counsellors, who will almost certainly find that there are a substantial number of 13-15 year olds on their books. The reasons for referral may not necessarily be very different from the reasons for referral for 10-13 year olds, but the children's pre-occupations usually are, and the counsellor's approach needs to change a little. She needs, for example, to understand the adolescent drive towards independence, and the way in which this can conflict with parental needs and expectations. She also needs to understand the acute sensitivity of adolescents, who may *look* tough, whilst being at heart vulnerable, anxious, and low in self-esteem.   Since it is a time of life when, occasionally, quite serious personality and psychiatric problems such as depression or anorexia nervosa appear, the counsellor must also be alert to the possibility that some of her clients may need more expert help than she is able to offer.

Dealing with adolescent children, the counsellor will have to take account of her clients' increased interest in sex and sexual relationships. At the same time, she will become aware that the subject is not necessarily of prime importance to *all* of her clients, some of whom (particularly, perhaps, boys) are still more interested in proving themselves and forming relationships with their like-sex peers. On this as on most subjects the counsellor takes her cues from her clients. She may ask a child if he or she has a girlfriend/boyfriend, and the child's answer will almost certainly give her a clue as to whether it is a subject worth pursuing, or not.

Occasionally - though not, in my experience, so very often - she will become aware that one of her young clients is having a sexual relationship with another person, probably of the same age-group. She may well feel uncertain as to whether the child's parents should be told. In most cases she will probably want to discuss this with the child and perhaps persuade her (the situation is particularly acute with girls, for obvious reasons) that underage sex is not a good idea, and that her parents should know of it. However, the counsellor is probably unlikely to override the child's wishes if she states firmly that she does not want her parents to be informed of her behaviour.

Sticking it out

For some young people, the period of time between 14 and 16 is almost intolerable, particularly if their families are not supportive or if their parents have so many problems of their own that they have no time for their children. All too often, children have to fend for themselves, physically and emotionally, long before they are ready to stand on their own two feet.

No doubt this was always so, yet one has a feeling that in the current climate of opinion, where adults (i.e parents) expect to further their own interests and seek fulfilment for themselves at a time of life when in the past they would simply have accepted their lot as parents, this does not help. Parents become disenchanted with each other and discontented with their lives; marriages break up and new liaisons are made - and all at a times when the children need stability, continuity, affection and a good measure of sensible discipline.

Time and again, those who counsel children will find themselves providing the "secure base" which children need, whilst parents seem to be shirking their own responsibilities. Nevertheless, children love their parents and rarely wish to leave them, however unsupportive the home may seem to be. On rare occasions, a counsellor may become aware that life for a young client at home is not merely insecure, but positively and fundamentally damaging to his well-being. On such occasions, the counsellor may have to take a decision as to whether or not it is appropriate to approach the social services with a view to asking them to take action on a child's behalf.

Opinions will differ on this matter, and each case is different. However, children of 14 or 15 years of age are old enough to take part in a sensible conversation with their counsellors about the advantages and disadvantages of such a move. Most can talk about their own feelings and experiences with a counsellor whom they have come to know and trust and, with her help, decide whether or not it is possible to "stick it out" until they are old enough to leave school and make their own way in the world. Counsellors, for their part, should recognise the importance of discouraging children from taking any rash steps. Experience tells them that there are few substitute parents available for adolescent children, and that life in Care is not necessarily a happy one. A few years spent putting up with difficult circumstances may in the long run prove to be the best option for the child.

CHAPTER FIVE

CHILDREN IN DISTRESS

In recent years there has been an increased awareness of the part which counsellors can play in helping children who have experienced trauma or loss, or have been physically or sexually abused. The number of children who need help is considerable, and there will probably never be enough trained counsellors to meet their needs. Certain voluntary agencies such as "Childline" make an important contribution. At the same time, those who work as school counsellors, or in the child psychological or psychiatric services, or in certain sections of the social services, do their best to provide the necessary opportunities for children who need their help.

Children who are in distress occasionally ask for help, perhaps approaching their teachers or another sympathetic adult outside the family. More frequently, perhaps, there is information available from various sources which suggests that a child is in some way at risk. Sometimes a child's manner, perhaps at school, suggests that he is desperately unhappy. Occasionally, a parent recognises that their child is confused or unhappy (say, following a divorce) and seeks counselling help for him.

The counselling of distressed children is rather different from the counselling of troublesome children. We have, of course, seen in preceding chapters that troublesome children can also be distressed. However, there are differences between counselling a child whose behaviour is giving cause for concern (whatever the reason for it) and counselling a child whose distress is openly recognised, or who is known to be at risk in some way.

Whatever the nature of the problem, however, the counsellor always needs her basic counselling skills. She knows the value of providing the child with an opportunity to talk: the space, and the secure base which he needs to be able to communicate his thoughts and feelings freely. She listens attentively, and indicates that she takes the child seriously. From time to time, she will ask a question to clarify certain points for herself and to encourage the child to express himself clearly. She needs to show sympathy and understanding, and to avoid looking shocked or dismayed. At the same time she needs to try to obtain a relatively accurate picture of the situation which is causing the child's distress.

Sometimes a counsellor needs particular tact and sensitivity, for example if she is interviewing a child who, it is alleged, has been sexually abused. Such a child was Karen, aged 9.

THE CASE OF KAREN

Karen lives with her mother in a small maisonette. Her father has left them and lives with another woman a few miles away. He remains on good terms with Karen's mother, and sees Karen on a regular basis, though infrequently.

Karen's mother is an attractive young woman, and she forms a relationship with Don, who is a year or two younger than she. He does not live with them, but visits regularly, and spends the night with Karen's mother occasionally. He also looks after Karen one evening a week while her mother attends an evening class. During one of these evenings, according to Karen, Ken "puts his hand up" her skirt and "touches my bottom".

The counsellor comes into the picture when Karen tells an aunt, her mother's sister, of Don's behaviour. The aunt has approached the social services department, and it is the counsellor's task to see Karen and to try and discover exactly what has taken place. Don himself has denied "interfering with" Karen.

In the counsellor's room, Karen sits rather awkwardly on the edge of her chair. She is a neat, pretty child, with dark curls and a rather nervous smile. The counsellor asks her if she knows why she is there. Karen looks uncomfortable, and says nothing.

Counsellor: "I think you must know, Karen, that you are here because of what you told Auntie Penny the other day, about Don. I understand that it may be rather embarrassing to talk about it".

Karen nods, but remains silent.

Counsellor: "Can you tell me what you told your Auntie Penny?"

Karen fidgets a little.

Counsellor: "You see, it is rather important that we know just what happened. (She pauses) Don is mummy's boyfriend. Is that right?"

Karen: "Yes".

Counsellor: "And he sometimes looks after you when she goes out?"

Karen: "Yes. When she goes to evening class, mostly".

Counsellor: "I see. And how do you get on with Don?"

Karen crinkles he nose, and hesitates. He's "all right", she says. Then, after a brief pause, her face crumples and she is near to tears. Why, she asks, does he keep touching her?

With a little more encouragement,Karen tells the counsellor about the regular abuse which has, fortunately, not been more than "touching". The counsellor listens sympathetically, not saying much. She knows that it is important not to step in too quickly now that Karen has begun to talk, nor to show indignation or anger, however much she may feel it. At this point, the most important thing is to acquire factual information in a simple and straightforward manner.

When Karen is a little calmer, the counsellor asks her to tell her more about Don. Has he been behaving towards her like this for a long time? Karen says no. At first, she had liked him. They had watched television together, and it was good because he let her stay up later than Mummy did. The late bedtime was their "secret". No doubt, Don hoped that Karen would also keep silent about his sexual advances.

Later in the session, the counsellor tells Karen that she was right to tell her aunt about Don's behaviour. But why had she not told her mother? Karen bites her lips and seems uncertain. She is silent again.

Counsellor (after a short pause): "Tell me about your mum. Do you and she get on well together?"

Karen: "It's OK. Sometimes we quarrel".

Counsellor: "Sometimes she gets cross with you?".

Karen: "When I'm naughty".

Counsellor: "And what do you do that is naughty?"

Karen: "Sometimes I'm cheeky. (she pauses) And she gets cross when I don't keep my bedroom tidy".

Counsellor: "Mmmm, I see. (A pause) Can you tell me abut your Dad?"

Karen: "What about him? He doesn't live with us any more". (Her manner is defensive.)

Counsellor: "I know. He left home quite some time ago, I believe".

Karen: "Yes".

Counsellor: "I should think that you probably miss him a bit".

Karen: "No". (Then after a pause) "Yes".

Her face is rather red and angry. She tells the counsellor about her visits to her father which she dislikes because the woman with whom he now lives is unsympathetic. There are certain small, but unimportant matters which have also upset Karen, such as a forgotten birthday. As is so often the case, the matter is complicated - more complicated than it appeared at first sight. The counsellor knows that there is much work to be done, but is also aware that for the time being at least she must return to the subject which led to her meeting with Karen. She tells Karen that she understands that life has been quite difficult for her over the last few years, and that she was right to tell others about what Don had done. He was wrong to touch her in this way, and people would be taking action to ensure that it does not happen again.

It is worth remembering that the counsellor's reassurance to children like Karen must be adapted to the circumstances of the case. In Karen's case, the counsellor felt sure that there was enough information, and that Karen's mother was sensible enough, to ensure that appropriate action would be taken to protect her. However, in some cases a counsellor would not feel so confident about the outcome. And it is, of course, extremely unhelpful to children to make predictions or promises when the future seems unclear. This includes promising to see a child again, unless the counsellor is sure she will be in a position to do so.

Investigation of abuse

An initial interview with a child who has complained of sexual (or other) abuse, such as the one outlined above, is only the beginning of what is usually a lengthy process of investigation by the police and social services department. Each case is different, and the outcome depends partly on the behaviour of adults close to the child: for example, on whether or not the abuse is admitted, and whether the alleged abuser is a family member. It also depends on the way in which the local child protection services are organised. Those involved will discuss the matter and a decision may need to be taken about whether the child should be removed from her home, on a short-term or a long-term basis. Further investigations may reveal a general lack of adequate parental care, which suggests that the child might be better off away from his family. On the other hand, the home circumstances may, as in Karen's case, be fundamentally quite good, and no such drastic step need be taken.

In all cases of alleged abuse, work with the child and family is needed, and is designed to suit the needs of the case. It will probably be undertaken by someone who has had training in family therapy. At the same time, those concerned in the case will need to take a decision about what action should be taken against the alleged abuser. The counsellor may be - should be - involved in the discussions and the decision-making process, although her opinion will, of course, be only one of many.

Sexual and physical abuse of children is a painful and distressing matter, which arouses strong feelings in adults. A Counsellor who is involved in such cases needs the advice and support of others (see below and in later chapters). She also needs to be aware of her own part in the scheme of things. She may, as in the case of Karen, become aware that there are other difficulties in a child's life or, indeed, feel that she is not getting a clear picture of what has, or has not, happened. At times, she will feel angry with others, who seem unable to offer the child the protection he seems to need.

Counsellors who work with distressed children need to know the limitations of their work. Children who have been sexually or physically abused over a long period of time may need the help of others, such as child psychotherapists, for many months or even years.

Stress in the family

Probably the single most important cause of distress in children is serious disruption or violence in the family (not necessarily towards the child himself). Admittedly disruption and even violence is a way of life for a number of families, and many children manage to rise above it. However, for some it is an almost impossible emotional burden to bear. The disruption and conflict touches children in different ways. For some, there is fear and anger at seeing one parent brow-beaten or misused by the other; for others it may be the feeling of guilt, as if the child himself were in some way to blame for the parents' problems. And many children feel the conflict of divided loyalties as parents pull in opposite directions, creating chaos for the family as a whole.

Children who live in difficult home situations can often learn to come to terms with their family's (and their parents') inadequacies, and develop skills of their own which take them into adult life quite successfully, particularly if they have reached the age of adolescence. In many cases, particularly with older children, the counsellor can help by combining a sympathetic understanding for the child's predicament with encouragement and advice about how to behave, look after oneself, keep out of trouble, detach oneself from the family difficulties. Once the child has found it possible to communicate, and has the experience of feeling that someone understands and is willing to help, he or she may even begin to understand the parental viewpoint, and to accept the difficulties that have been in the family with greater equanimity. However, this state of mind is not necessarily quickly achieved.

THE CASE OF PAULINE

The case of Pauline (aged 15) illustrates how a child can be helped to live with distressing home circumstances and to grow in spite of them. It comes from her teacher who, while on a counselling course, was becoming increasingly worried about her at school, describing her as "lost, absent, with very poor concentration, unwilling to participate in activities, defeatist". Eventually, after she had decided to approach Pauline to ask about these things, Pauline approaches her herself:

In the afternoon of that very day Pauline approached me. I started seeing her from the following day and I continued to see her, bar absences, till the end of the school year. Pauline was indeed in desperate need of help. Her state of mind was like that of someone nearing a mental breakdown. I was surprised that she had been coping the way she had for such a long time, considering the circumstances.

There was a background of violence in her home life. Her father was an alcoholic with a tendency to behave violently. There were regular arguments and scenes in the family with much shouting and unhappiness. Pauline's two older sisters were working; her mother was not working. There was no communication with any member of the family besides the pattern of quarrels and bickerings; no proper eating or sleeping patterns.

Pauline had deep feelings of hatred against her father, and was convinced that her mother did not love her or care about her. She had a deep sense of helplessness rooted in early childhood; since at the age of 5 she witnessed violent attacks on her mother by her drunken father; she had been there, watching it all and not being able to help.

At each session Pauline talked very freely. She told me a lot about herself, her mother, father, sisters and friends, as if she had been waiting for such an opportunity for ages, pouring out all her troubles and her emotions. She cried, and spoke of her feelings of sorrow, resentment, love, guilt, helplessness, fear. Sometimes she laughed or swore.

Pauline seemed to be in a state of utter confusion. After the "unloading" period, we started to pick up the pieces, looking carefully at each problem in turn and trying to establish a sort of priority. I set out to build her feelings of self-worth, and to strengthen her feelings of identity by encouraging her to describe her own interests. It seemed important to help her see that she was a valuable individual, a person in her own right who needed to care about herself. We therefore discussed the need to look after oneself, have regular meals and regular hours of sleep.

I also felt it was necessary to strengthen the family bond, and tried to encourage her to think more positively about her mother and her two working sisters. It seemed important to consider small matters, and to help Pauline think how she could improve the situation at home, however slightly. She told me on one occasion that she had made a cup of tea for her mother - an important event in a family in which each member had the habit of dealing only with his or her own needs (i.e. cooking, washing up).

By building up Pauline's personal identity and feelings of self-worth, I seemed to be able to help her become more relaxed and confident. The sessions ceased to have the same urgency. Gradually, Pauline became quite proud to relate the little things she had done, the small improvements in her life. Some of these improvements were personal, others were in connection with acts of co-operation in the family as a whole.

It took me longer to help Pauline grasp a realistic, deep understanding of her father's predicament, and to think about her feelings of hate towards him. She did however begin to talk more realistically about her feelings of guilt and of anger, rather than laughing hysterically every time she mentioned anything to do with him, as she had done in earlier sessions.

It seems to me that in this case we are given insight into the way in which a counsellor can help a child come to terms with a family situation which he cannot change, without encouraging the child to reject the family completely. Pauline was helped to see that she was an important individual with her own strengths of personality, her own likes and dislikes, her own feelings and experiences. Once she was calmer, and had more confidence in herself, she could also begin to understand the predicament of other members of her family. As she begins to understand their separate points of view, the chaotic anguish fades, and Pauline can begin to see that her parents' problems belong to *them* and need not overwhelm *her*. Little by little, she can begin to make a normal life for herself.

Loss

The occasional loss of loved ones, and the suffering which this entails, is an unavoidable part of the human experience. During childhood, the most common loss is that of a parent through separation or divorce. Family splits are now so common that we risk overlooking the fact that they are always a source of suffering to the children concerned.

When a family breaks up, however gracefully from the adults' point of view, the children lose a parent. It may well be that in the long run the divorce or separation is a good thing for all concerned, but for the time being there is the painful reality that a loved parent (usually the father) is no longer present. Some parents try to put a gloss on the situation, saying that "nothing has changed" or "the children still see their father", but visits, outings and treats cannot substitute for daily contact with someone whom one loves. It is possible to get over it, but the loss is painful, often for a long time.

The death of a close relative is a less common experience for a child and brings with it suffering of a rather different nature. Death is final and the person will not be seen again. There is also incomprehensibility about it that affects us all, and children are no exceptions. Like adults, they need to grieve and to come to terms with their loss; like adults, they may find it difficult to accept. They can also become confused if other people speak as if the person who has died is "still with us" or "has fallen asleep". Expressions of this nature, helpful to some adults, can create difficulties for a child who is trying to face up to the reality of death.

The death of a loved one is often associated with feelings of guilt or anger. For children, there may be a feeling that one's naughty behaviour was in some way damaging to the person who has died, and might have contributed to the death. Religious beliefs, helpful to some, can be a source of anguish to others.

Counsellors need to be aware of the many and complex feelings which children can have, following the departure or death of a loved relative. Tact and sensitivy are needed, and the Counsellor should avoid assuming that she knows "how the child feels". It is perhaps most helpful to ask one or two straightforward questions about the lost person. Are there some photographs which the child might like to bring to the next session? Is there some particular event which he might like to talk about?

A conversation with a child which starts in a rather matter-in-fact way like this may well lead him to express feelings of sadness or anger to the counsellor. It may also encourage a child to ask questions which he does not feel able to ask his parents. The counsellor, for her part, takes her cue from the child. If he wants to talk, she is ready to listen; if not, she respects his need for silence.

Occasionally a counsellor becomes aware that a child's experience of loss is proving particularly stressful so that she feels that other help may be needed. In these cases, it is important to get in touch with the parent(s), who may also need counselling. A referral to another agency (see Chapter Eleven) may be indicated.

Taking action

Children in distress always benefit from an opportunity to talk about their circumstances and their feelings, whether or not it is possible to change the conditions that are making them unhappy or fearful. Experienced counsellors are aware of this. They are also keenly aware of the differences between counselling and taking action to help a child.

Counsellors need to know how to allow a child to communicate and express his feelings and how to "hold on to" these feelings for him, without giving him the impression that something will be done on his behalf. However sad or angry one feels, or however one may wish to take action on a particular child's behalf, it is always necessary to reflect on difficult cases and discuss them with others who are appropriately trained before making any moves towards trying to change the circumstances of a child's life.

It may well be that in some cases, a child's family circumstances need investigation and in a few cases, a child will need to be removed from his family. It may also be occasionally that legal actions will be taken against adults, who may or may not be members of the child's family. These decisions will not be taken by the counsellor herself, although she may have a part in the decision-making.

These matters are discussed in greater detail in Chapter Eleven.

CHAPTER SIX

THE TRUTH OF THE MATTER

In her work with children, the counsellor hears many things which may or may not be true. She accepts that much of what her young clients tell her will probably be to some extent distorted to suit the needs of the moment. However, she is aware that in the long run, this will not necesssarily affect her ability to help the child. She also knows that there is little to be gained by putting pressure on a child to be more precise or by challenging him as to the truth of certain statements.

Occasionally, however, it is important to try and establish the truth. Certain things may be said during the course of a session with a child which the counsellor feels she cannot let pass without seeking information of a more detailed nature. A statement from a child that his father hits him may or may not indicate a serious state of affairs, but it makes the counsellor think that she should ask for further details. The way in which she does this depends on many things: the age of the child, how well she knows him, her general impression of his health and well-being. If she decides to pursue the matter, she is aware of the need for caution. She might perhaps ask how often he is hit, and with what. If it seems appropriate, she may ask if there are any marks or bruises, now or at any time, which he would like to show her or tell her about. If his replies indicate that there is cause for concern, the counsellor will probably want to discuss the matter with a colleague with a view to deciding whether it is appropriate to take further action, and, if so, what action should be taken.

Direct statements from children indicating that they are being physically chastised at home are difficult to deal with since there is usually no way of establishing the exact truth of the matter, nor any clear line between what is, and is not, acceptable chastisement. Expressions of feeling can be even more awkward. "I hate my stepfather" may or may not indicate a serious problem of abuse. Tactful questioning may reveal that there is cause for alarm and need for intervention, but it may not. Indeed, it is more than likely that the child's dislike of the stepfather reflects his sadness at the loss of his natural father. Perhaps the stepfather is attempting to establish a measure of discipline in his new family but this does not necessarily mean that he is abusing its younger members. Again, there is need for caution on the part of the counsellor.

Asking questions

A counsellor is sometimes in possession of certain information about a child before she meets him. It may be that the referring adult has good reasons to suspect that the child is being abused, and that the counsellor has been asked to see the child with these thoughts in mind. In these circumstances, the counsellor will need to be fairly direct with the child, once she has established reasonable contact with him. How she does this is a matter of personal judgement. If she does not feel that it is useful to say exactly what she has been told, she may tell him that other people are worried about him, and about what might be happening to him. Is there anything disagreeable or frightening that someone is doing to him that he should tell her about? Is anyone behaving badly, or upsetting him?

With older children, she may find it helpful to ask the child if he knows what is meant by physical or sexual abuse. His answer may not be very clear, but it should give the counsellor some indication as to whether he has an understanding of what is meant. It also helps her to decide just how direct her next questions should be.

Direct questioning based on the assumption that the child is in possession of information of a damaging nature which must be revealed is always difficult for the counsellor, since it invites the child to make complaints about the behaviour of other people. Once the allegations are made, the matter cannot be left. It is therefore essential for the counsellor to establish the truth if she possibly can. It is also important for her to be able to be honest if she feels she has *not* heard the truth.

The experienced counsellor knows that there are always many possible reasons why a child may be feeling unhappy or behaving in a troubled manner. She knows that it is necessary to keep an open mind when asking questions, and to ask them in a calm and neutral manner. Children are sensitive to adult expectations and more likely to be influenced by certain nuances in the adult voice than adults. In an important matter, when it is essential to obtain the truth, the Counsellor must be wary of putting her questions to the child in a manner which sugests to him what his answers might be.

A delicate task

This is not an easy subject. There is no clear path for a counsellor who is trying to investigate a case where a child may be suffering from neglect or abuse to follow. Each case is different, and the counsellor must use her judgement, tact and expertise in choosing the right words at the right moment in each case. She knows that many of the children she sees are living in difficult and stressful circumstances, but is also aware that this does not mean that they are being abused. She is aware, too, that her ability to help a child depends very much on her openness and willingness to listen, rather than on her ability to develop the skills of cross-examination! In cases of possible sexual abuse, there is also some danger that the well-meaning though inexperienced counsellor can tread too heavily into an area which is, for the pre-adolescent child, still essentially mysterious and full of promise.

Occasionally, and painfully, a counsellor will be aware that a child is deliberately withholding information from her, probably to protect someone else. The session is awkward, the child evasive or even totally silent, and the counsellor feels frustrated and inadequate. However, even an apparently unsatisfactory interview can often be helpful to a child, if he leaves with the impression that it is possible to communicate and that there are people who are willing to listen. On another occasion, he may make better use of the opportunity.

Do children always tell the truth?

It is worth remembering that at one time, and until relatively recently, it was customary to view the comments of children with suspicion. Nowadays, there is a generally held belief that children are unlikely to tell lies about serious matters. In practice, the position is far from straightforward. Though most children are probably a good deal more honest than most adults, their ability and willingness to tell the truth on any given occasion cannot necessarily be guaranteed.

Clearly, a child's age is important, and the younger the child the greater the need for caution before placing confidence in the truthfulness and accuracy of his assertions. A very young child may not necessarily have an intention to deceive, but he is prone to certain misconceptions and likely to be confused by adult questioning. Young children may also be inclined to give an answer which they feel is expected of them, rather than trying to be accurate and truthful. Many also have a rather limited, and in some respects special and idiosyncratic, vocabulary, making it hard for the adult who does not know the child to understand exactly what he means. Great care is needed, therefore, when discussing delicate and personal matters with children under the age of about 5 or 6 years, and the younger the child the greater the need for care. It is at least arguable that the counselling of very young children should only be undertaken by someone who has had particular experience in working with them. If she has not had this experience, the counsellor may need the advice and support of, say, a child psychotherapist, or a psychologist who has had experience with this age group.

Between the age of about 6 and 12 years, children tend to be basically straightforward and, with a few exceptions, comprehensible. They are, unless they are of low ability (I.Q.) or seriously emotionally disturbed, well aware of the difference between fantasy and reality and between right and wrong. On the other hand, they are not usually much inclined to introspection and reflection. Some may also be influenced by feelings of loyalty, embarrassment and anxiety about the consequences of talking about their experiences. Occasionally, they choose to keep silent, which makes things very difficult for the counsellor who is aware - or at least half aware - that all is not as it should be in the child's life.

At around adolescence, a greater sense of personal responsibility linked with a desire for self-protection emerges, and children who accepted their lot in life without complaint may begin to realise that they do not need to continue to do this. At adolescence, the abused child may suddenly turn on the exploiting adult, or "tell", or even run away from home. At the same time, the feelings of love and loyalty to family members do not disappear and the child may suffer considerable internal conflict. It is not uncommon to hear 13-14 year olds express both love and hate of parents, almost in the same breath. Nor is it unusual for the counsellor to hear at one session that the child wants to leave home (for example, to go into Care) and at the next that he does not.

The adult influence

Children are inevitably, influenced by their past experiences of adult behaviour, and this will also affect the way in which they respond to the counsellor. It is difficult for a child who has lived with adults who have not communicated directly with him, nor kept their promises, to accept that most adults mean what they say and say what they mean. Difficult, too, for a child who has experienced angry adult responses for relatively trivial misdemeanours to put their thoughts into words directly and confidently. Such children may well take refuge in silence, lie-telling or exaggeration, rather than giving a simple account of themselves and their experiences.

Counsellors need to be aware that many of the troubled and unhappy children they see have not had the opportunity to confide in a sensible and affectionate adult, and that they may well have great difficulty in trusting the counsellor. Fear and uncertainty can prompt a child to give a quick, untruthful reply to a question, which he may not feel able to retract at a later stage. It is always important to avoid putting pressure on a child. Not only can he not be made to reveal things against his wish, but the pressure may in fact prevent him from telling the adult those things which need to be told.

CHAPTER SEVEN

ILLNESS AND DISABILITY

In spite of the greatly improved health of children over the past 20 or 30 years, and the advances of medical science, a certain number of children must still bear with chronic illness, or with physical disabilities which fundamentally limit their activities and opportunities. In some cases, the illness or disabilities have serious long-term implications, and may even be associated with deterioration to an early death. More often, they are not life-threatening but impair the quality of life for the child to a greater or lesser extent.

Some children must put up with conditions which make their lives substantially different from those of their peers. There are children who must, for example, wear hearing aids or callipers, or ride in a wheel chair, and those who suffer from paralysis or deformity of a limb. The conditions themselves vary in their severity, but they are not usually amenable to treatment and will be, to a greater or lesser extent, a source of anguish or embarrassment to a child throughout his life. Children can, of course, learn to come to terms with it, and many children manage to lead full lives in spite of their disabilities.

Children with chronic and serious illnesses such as cystic fibrosis, coeliac disease, kidney disease, heart and respiratory disorders, have rather different problems with which to contend. Outwardly, they may look like other children, although their medical conditions impose certain limitations on them. They may also need to spend long periods of time undergoing investigations and suffering the discomfort or pain of certain essential medical treatments. They often miss periods of schooling, and spend much of their time feeling debilitated.

Some children need regular hospital treatment, involving

perhaps several admissions for surgery, or for certain medical procedures such as blood transfusion. Children who suffer from certain diseases such as leukemia may need to undergo bone marrow transplantation, a lengthy and uncomfortable procedure, the success of which cannot be guaranteed.

Children who suffer from chronic and disabling conditions can benefit considerably from a counsellor's help. However, the counsellor must have a working knowledge of the children's medical/physical conditions and disabilities, if she is to work with the children effectively. A good deal of suffering and embarrassment can arise if the counsellor is not aware of the outlook for each child, or of the limitations which his disability or illness impose upon him. This is a specialist field, where there is considerable potential for the counsellor who is willing to acquire the necessary knowledge. It is indeed a rather different form of counselling, though one which still needs the basic counselling skills.

Although sick and disabled children benefit from an opportunity to share their feelings and experiences with others they may not always find this easy to do. Nor is it easy for fit and able-bodied people to contemplate the problems of being seriously disabled. Communication in a group (see following chapter) is often easier for everyone than counselling on an individual basis. Talking about themselves, with a counsellor's help, disabled children can learn from each other in a practical sense. They can also derive support and encouragement from each other.

Children in hospital

Relatively few children spend a long period of time in hospital nowadays, and those who do usually have serious and life-threatening conditions which need complex and expert medical attention, such as leukemia, chronic kidney disorders, cancer. Hospitals which specialise in the treatment of such serious conditions usually provide counselling and support services for the children and their families, and the people who provide these services develop considerable expertise.

There is also, however, a small but significant number of children who need to be admitted to hospital for short treatments of one kind or another. This would include children with disabilities who are admitted for a surgical procedure or for a brief, intensive medical treatment.which can improve some aspect of their lives, without curing the child. In these cases, the hospital may not provide counselling services. However, a counsellor working in other settings (e.g. a school) may find that some of her young clients have had these experiences, and wish to talk about them.

Counsellors who work regularly with sick children need to know something of the medical details. It is important to know what is planned for the child and what the outcome might be, in any particular case. The treatment may have a very limited purpose, and it is important that both counsellor and child are aware of this so that the child does not have any unrealistic expectations. The counsellor also needs to know of possible side effects (e.g. hair loss) of a particular medical treatment, so that she can prepare and support the child accordingly.

Modern medicine has brought new hope to many people, and a number of children are alive today with conditions which were not amenable to treatment even a short time ago (for example, some cases of childhood leukemia). However, there is still a limit to what can be achieved by even the most skilled and dedicated doctors and nurses. Counsellors who work with sick children need to be aware of this, and able to offer help on the basis of reality, rather than through false hopes and false expectations.

Respecting a child's feelings

One of the most difficult aspects of working with children who are living in situations from which they cannot escape is that of respecting the child's privacy and his own efforts to "cope" with a situation which he cannot change. On the one hand, we are aware of the value of talking about one's fears and anxieties; on the other, it may be more comfortable not to talk, or even to think, about certain painful realities.

It is certainly no part of the counsellor's brief to force children to talk about a subject which they do not wish to discuss, such as their own serious illness or disability. Sometimes it is more helpful to make a relationship with a child which is based on something he wants to do, or talk about, (a game, a story, an outing). During this friendly contact, the counsellor might find an opportunity to broach the more serious subject of his illness or disability but she will always want to exercise tact and respect a child's reticence. The counsellor who is experienced in this field learns how to broach with a child the painful subject of his illness in a manner that allows him to talk of it if he wishesor, if he prefers, to keep silent.

In some circumstances sick or disabled children should be given direct and factual information. Children who must undergo painful surgical procedures, suffer injections, take disagreeable medicines, need to be given a reason for the treatment. They also need to be told in advance roughly what to expect. Honesty on the part of the adults allows the child to develop confidence in those who are treating him. If he is told, in substance "this will hurt a little/taste disagreeable/make you feel rather sore .. but it is necessary to make you better", he may complain or even cry, but he will probably accept the procedures without too much fuss. He will also accept subsequent treatment in a trusting manner. His fortitude needs to be recognised openly, and praised by the adults involved. He also needs constant adult encouragement and support, particularly if the treatment is lengthy. In many cases, this will be offered by the parents, but a counsellor can have an important part to play.

The seriously ill and dying child

Children who are seriously ill are, like most adults in a similar position, usually aware of their predicament. Like adults, some do and some do not ask questions about their illness and its likely outcome. Again, the counsellor needs to be sensitive to the child's feelings, and to the things he says, or asks, before talking about the seriousness of his condition to him.

Opinions differ in this field as to whether an individual who is facing death should be told of this. Some doctors feel that it is important to prepare the patient; others feel that the truth should be kept from him. Much will depend on his state of alertness. If a child is heavily sedated, or so ill that he is out-of-touch with his surroundings, any form of discussion or explanation is obviously inappropriate. He needs someone to stay with him holding his hand until his life comes to an end. If he is more alert, the counsellor may want to talk with him and his parents about the seriousness of his condition and, perhaps, his impending death. Fortunately counsellors who work in this specialised field will not have to take these difficult decisions alone. Almost certainly they will be part of a team which has a policy on these matters.

Thinking about siblings

In families where there is a chronically ill or disabled child, there are quite often healthy brothers and sisters whose positions needs to be considered sympathetically. Such children often have their own burden to bear. In many cases there will be feelings of guilt as they observe the predicament of their brother or sister and begin to understand that there is no hope of change. There may be a feeling that it is necessary to be very "good", supportive to the parents and tolerant of any idiosyncrasies which the disabled or sick child might have and of the attention which the parents give him. It can be difficult for a child to live for many years in the position of being a "helper" to the parent, and of suppressing his own needs and feelings.

Death is uncommon in children, but when it occurs, siblings can, of course, suffer greatly from the loss. Unfortunately, their needs can be overlooked. Indeed, their suffering may not be expressed openly, since the child fears to upset the parents further. Occasionally, bottled-up emotions can lead to depression, or to troubled behaviour in a child.

On relatively rare occasions, a sibling is required to make some direct contribution to the treatment of the sick child. The best example of this is the donation of bone marrow when a sibling has compatible tissue which can be used to replace the sick child's malfunctioning bone marrow. For the sibling, this is not a particularly painful procedure, but it does involve a brief admission to hospital, undergoing anaesthetic and feeling sore for a few days on the site chosen to extract the bone marrow. The situation has, however, its own unusual and potentially stressful quality. The sibling suffers for the sake of the sick child, and the sick child, for his part, owes his life to his sibling. And if, as sometimes happens, the transplant fails, there is the possibility of further stress for the sibling. It is after all his tissue, and in a sense he himself, which has failed to help his brother.

The counsellor as part of a team.

The counsellor who is asked to help a sick child, or a child who seems to be experiencing stress because another person in the family is sick, needs to be able to co-operate fully with whoever else is involved. Medical requirements, and the opinions and wishes of the child's doctors and nurses are, of course, paramount. However, others will also be involved. It may be, for example, that a social-worker is attempting to provide practical help and support for the sick child and/or for the family as a whole. Sometimes other professional people such as psychologists, psychiatrists, speech therapists, physiotherapists etc., are involved as well. The counsellor needs to be clear in her mind as to her own contribution and responsibilities, while at the same time informing herself as to the contributions and opinions of others.

In this specialised field of counselling it is impossible to do more than indicate some aspects of a counsellor's work with children. Those who are interested in learning about "non-medical" aspects of caring for sick children might find it useful to read *The Other Side Of Paediatrics: A Guide To The Every-day Care Of Sick Children* (Jolly, J., Macmillan Educational Books, 1981).

CHAPTER EIGHT

GROUP COUNSELLING

Counsellors will usually be aware that the number of children who could benefit from their help is far greater than they could ever hope to deal with on an individual basis. Many junior school children have certain minor problems of social adjustment, and would benefit from the opportunity to think about themselves, their behaviour and their relationships with other people before transferring to secondary school. Older children can also benefit from counselling sessions designed to help them consider the problems which many children experience during adolescence. For this reason, counsellors may find that there is real advantage in developing methods of working with groups of children.

Groupwork brings the counsellor's expertise to a much greater number of children. It can also provide additional opportunities for promoting change, not available in individual sessions. For example, a counsellor who works with a group of children will almost certainly find that one or two are relatively forthcoming, and these children's contributions can be used to stimulate thought in more reticent children. Shy children benefit from seeing that it is possible to talk freely about yourself and your experiences, whilst more talkative children benefit from being encouraged to wait and listen to others. Ideas circulate, and the children learn from each other.

Working with her group, the counsellor aims to bring into the conversation those subjects which are important to the particular age group. She will hope to encourage the children to discuss a variety of different subjects, express their feelings openly, and consider ways of tackling familiar problems. She hopes that every child will join in and make his contribution.

At the same time, she realises that this is difficult for some children and will not want to pressurise a child.

Groupwork has many advantages, although there are certain disadvantages. Clearly, a counsellor cannot allow children to communicate intimate details of their lives in a group session, unless that group is run specifically for that purpose (e.g. a group which is run for sexually abused children). Some counsellors may also find that groupwork does not suit *them*, since it makes demands on them which individual sessions with children do not. For example, groupwork needs some structure and control from the adult, if the session is to be fruitful, and the counsellor needs to be confident that she can provide this.

Who can benefit?

All children can benefit from being part of a thoughtful group run by an adult counsellor who understands the normal and natural pre-occupations of childhood. However, some selection must be made since there are insufficient counsellors for all children to be offered groupwork. The adults concerned need therefore to have certain groups of children and certain possible problems in mind when planning the group.

Groupwork is extremely useful for children between the ages of about 8 and 11 who are somewhat lacking in the skills of social and personal competence which one hopes to see in junior school children. A well-run group, offered for a few weeks and held once a week, can make a difference to the children's general attitude and feelings of confidence. It can also increase their chances of transferring to secondary school successfully when the time comes.

Children who have already transferred to secondary school and seem to be lacking in confidence in the new setting can benefit from group counselling designed to help them share their feelings about their experiences, ask questions, and think about the ways in which they might tackle new problems. In this setting, a number of routine matters such as homework, discipline, clothing, getting on with other people, can usefully be discussed with the counsellor's help.

Given that so many children could benefit from a counselling group, the counsellor needs to be able to think clearly about what she can and cannot offer, and to whom. She needs to consider the group as a whole, so will be concerned to select children who will "fit in with" each other. The children should be roughly of the same age. There may, however, be differing views as to whether or not it is desirable to aim for a single sex, or a mixed sex group. My own view would be that the mixed group is best for junior school children, whilst secondary school children benefit more (on the whole) from a single sex group.

Children on the verge of puberty often feel very awkward in the company of those of the opposite sex. True, they must learn to overcome this - and, of course, most do. However, there is merit in separating the sexes when one is running a group for children between the ages of 12 and 15, if only because the development of girls and boys at this age proceeds at quite a different pace. There are of course individual variations, but most 13 year old girls are very much on the threshold of womanhood, whilst most boys of this age are still children.

Teachers as group counsellors

Group counselling fits comfortably into a school setting, and some teachers have had the opportunity to discover just how valuable counselling skills can be in the classroom. Some teachers manage to involve the class as a whole in sessions which are designed to encourage children to communicate, and consider their behaviour and relationships with other people. One teacher held a group session weekly for all of her class (10-11 year olds), which she called the "safe circle". The children put their desks to one side and sat in a circle, thus creating an atmosphere which was different from the rest of the school day. Certain subjects were aired, and certain games played, all of which were designed to increase children's confidence, self-awareness and awareness of the needs of others. The children responded well to the informality, and understood that what took place in the group was different to that which normally took place in the classroom.

A teacher who understands the benefit of group counselling will want to create the opportunity for it, but may not feel able to take the whole of the class at the same time. It should be possible to arrange for selected groups of children to be taken, while the rest of the class is engaged in other activities with another teacher. Much will depend on the way in which the school is organised and, of course, the attitude of the head of the school to the idea of group counselling for the children.

Teachers who are interested in holding counselling sessions need to bear in mind that there is a difference between holding a group session for counselling purposes and teaching a group of children. Teaching, of its nature, involves adult direction and control, and conversations between pupils and teachers have a purpose which is defined as part of the curriculum. Counselling, on the other hand, provides a much more open-ended opportunity to children, and a far greater freedom of expression. Here, there are no right answers and no solutions - merely an opportunity to think, share and explore certain feelings and experiences in the company of others.

Teachers have an advantage over other counsellors in that they are familiar with children and able to "hold together" a large group. They may, however, find it quite difficult to change from the rather directive manner of the class teacher who has certain clear goals in mind, to the more passive, accepting, relatively neutral manner of the counsellor. On the other hand, counsellors who are not teachers may find it difficult to engage, and hold the attention of, a group of lively children sufficiently to allow the counselling session to take place. Much depends on the individual circumstances and on the children themselves (some are more co-operative than others). However, the counsellor must feel comfortable with her group before any work can proceed. She may well decide that it is best to start with a few children (i.e. five or six) before moving on to working with a larger number. If she is unsure of herself, she may decide to work with another counsellor, sharing responsibility for the group.

The group identity

Once the counsellor has decided who will be in the group, she should set about defining the group's existence. Its identity and importance need to be established. Time, place of meeting and the way in which people will sit need to be specified simply and clearly at the start of the group's existence, and the pattern kept throughout the duration of the group. Children are best placed sitting in a circle, on chairs or cross-legged on the floor, with the counsellor a part of the circle. When everyone is present, it is helpful to maintain a brief silence to encourage people to turn their thoughts inwards and away from whatever activity they had been engaged in before the group session. Some counsellors use a brief routine "Close your eyes, finger tips together", for example, to mark the start of a group session with junior school children. However it is not essential. The important thing is to establish the group's existence, and its identity, as separate from other class activities. The starting and the finishing of each group session is made clear by the counsellor. Three quarters of an hour is enough for younger children, and an hour or an hour and a quarter for children of about 10+. Ideally, there should be no interruptions and people should not leave or join the group when it is in session.

The group in action

Taking a group of children for counselling, the counsellor needs the same basic skills as she needs for counselling individual children. She knows that she is providing the space and the secure base which the children need, in which they can express their feelings and describe their experiences. She knows, too, the importance of making each child feel respected and valued, even if what is said is sometimes unexpected, foolish or disagreeable.

Once a group has started, the children will make most of the running. However, the counsellor needs the creativity and the confidence to set the scene and, perhaps, to ask certain questions which stimulate thought. She will have certain themes in mind, relevant to the particular age group, and may introduce one of them herself. On the other hand, she may decide to let the children choose a subject.

Once a subject or theme seems to be emerging, the counsellor aims to focus the children's attention on it.

"Jenny seems to have been thinking quite hard about .....I wonder what others think".

"Terry has made an interesting suggestion. What would others do?"

This opens the discussion, whatever the topic, and the children are encouraged to make their contributions. The counsellor listens, quelling if necessary the more forceful children and making the minimum of comment herself. When a subject has been well aired, she will probably decide to round it off with a few quiet words before moving to something else.

Although counsellors like to encourage children to take the initiative, they sometimes find it valuable to set the ball roll ing themselves. A counsellor might say: "I've been thinking quite a bit recently about getting on with other people ......", leaving the sentence in the air. This approach, rather than one which says "Now, we are going to talk about ....", gives the children freedom to respond in a relaxed manner. Someone might ask "What do you mean?" or "Which other people?", giving an opportunity for others to say what they think is meant, and which people are being talked about. If there is no response at all (as there might be in a new group), the counsellor could carry on: "It seemed to me, as I was thinking about it, that it is often quite *hard* to get on with other people ...." The recognition that (a) the adult finds something hard and (b) that one can admit to finding something hard, is usually sufficient to start children talking.

As she talks and listens to the children the counsellor is keenly aware of each child as an individual, as well as of the group as a whole. It is as though an invisible thread links her to each child. When a child is talking, the counsellor looks at him and uses his name, and if a child is referred to by others, she again uses his name. This personal touch is essential if the children are to feel involved in the group and to benefit from the experience. The counsellor needs, therefore, to ensure that her group is of a manageable size, and does not contain more children than she can hold comfortably in mind. It is important not only to be able to remember each child's name, but to keep in mind his personal needs, strengths and weaknesses.

A group drawing

Not all children talk freely and it is sometimes helpful if the group can be engaged in a task which facilitates conversation. A group drawing is a valuable means of stimulating thought, and is particularly useful for younger junior school children (i.e. 7 - 9 year olds). A sheet of paper large enough for all the children to share and a plentiful supply of felt tip pens are all that are needed. It is useful to tell the children that they will be meeting to do this on, say, four occasions, at the same time and place.

A group drawing can only really be undertaken by seven or eight children, who should sit around the paper in a rough circle, so that they can see each other. The counsellor is part of the group, but does not herself usually draw (adults' drawings tend to be inhibiting to children). It is suggested quietly and without emphasis that the children might like to draw. Those who ask what they should draw are told: "Anything you like". Initially, some children will probably hesitate. One or two will start quite quickly, and before long the others join in. It is rare indeed for any child to remain aloof for long.

The joint drawing - which is not expected to be a work of art - serves several purposes. In one way, it is rather like a joint effort in "doodling" - a relaxing and undemanding activity which stimulates thought and conversation. It is also a social experience which the counsellor can use to advantage. There is, for example, an opportunity to comment on the way children share (or fail to share) the pens, take more than their fair share of paper, encroach on other people's space or interfere with another's drawings. The children's attention is drawn quite gently to these things: "Tracy seems to be taking quite a number of pens...." "Has Andrew got enough room, I wonder?"

The children's drawings also give the counsellor an indication of their pre-occupations and interests. She is carefully neutral, or mildly appreciative: "That is an interesting animal, David. Can you tell us about it?" "Is that your own house, Mary?" However, she avoids making too many personal comments about the children's drawings, and does not try to attribute any deeper meanings to them.

Sometimes children will co-operate with each other as they draw, so that a theme emerges. More often, perhaps, the drawings remain relatively separate (at least with younger children). At the end of the session the counsellor can invite comments from the children and the paper is turned round to facilitate inspection. The children are usually surprisingly positive about each other's efforts, asking interested questions and making friendly comments. The counsellor herself may want to add a few words. Perhaps she sees a theme emerging? If so, she might use this later with the group, as a focus for discussion.

Room for more negative feelings

We have seen in earlier chapters that counselling provides individual children with an opportunity to be more open and honest than usual, and to express their more negative feelings in the knowledge that they will be respected. Group counselling should provide children with a similar opportunity, should they wish to take it. However, negative feelings, though hard to bear, can be surprisingly difficult to express openly. Counsellors need to be aware of this and able to take account of it whilst working with the children.

The expression of negative feelings in a group may be even more difficult than it is on an individual basis, perhaps because of embarrassment or because there is a feeling that too much anger or despair might be intolerable. Yet it is particularly valuable for these feelings to be expressed in a situation where others are listening, and all can learn that such feelings are common to everyone. It is also valuable if individuals can learn how other people have managed to come through a crisis that resembles their own, or have learnt to control their feelings in difficult situations.

Counsellors should be able to give their clients permission to feel angry, unhappy, out-of-sorts, jealous, etc., by introducing these ideas into a group session. It may, for example, be possible to have an "I don't like" time, and invite children to contribute their own pet hates. "What makes me angry" is another possible theme, to which many children like to contribute. However, the counsellor should be aware of the need to avoid encouraging the expression of false feelings. There should be no obligation on individual children to contribute if they do not feel able to.

Counsellors should also feel able to encourage (or at least to accept) the communication of unhappy events and experiences. Children should feel that they can describe an unhappy event - perhaps the death of a loved animal - to others, and to have their feelings respected. It is all too easy for adults to brush aside these painful incidents, yet they are intensely important to the child concerned. They are also important in a more general sense, since they are part of the reality of life, which children must learn to accept.

Children with special needs

Children with certain particular and unusual problems (e.g. a severe hearing loss or other physical disability) can benefit considerably from a group designed particularly for them. It will need to be run by a counsellor who understands the children's disabilities. She may also need certain specific skills (e.g. the ability to use sign language in the case of a group of children with severe hearing loss). If the counsellor herself does not have the necessary specialised knowledge, she may consider working with a teacher who does, and who is sympathetic with her ideas.

Group counselling for children with a special need (handicap, disability) should provide scope for the children to discuss the problems associated with their physical condition. This will almost certainly lead to a discussion of the way in which a child with a handicap or disability feels in his relationship with other children who do not have the same problems. Much sadness or anger may be expressed at the way in which the world at large fails to understand, and provide for, the needs of disabled people.

Counsellors need particular skills for this work. They know that the children benefit from talking about their problems which are often considerable and hard to bear. At the same time, the counsellor knows that it is necessary to encourage the children to develop their inner resources, and their ability to cope with their difficulties. She will, therefore, aim to encourage the children to share ideas about how to get on with others, make the most of their opportunities, overcome their particular handicap or disability in so far as this is possible. She will also aim to help the children expand their ideas, and consider subjects which are not related to their disabilities.

As with the counselling of sick children (see Chapter Seven), this is a specialist field, too complex to consider in detail here.

The "learning support" group

Some children, not fundamentally disabled, nevertheless have certain difficulties with their school work. One thinks, for example, of the 7-9 year olds who have acute difficulties with reading (known in some quarters as "dyslexia"), and associated problems with writing and spelling. Such children should be receiving extra help and tuition at school. They can also benefit from group counselling.

Children who have failed to learn the basic skills of reading and writing alongside their peers are often lacking in confidence, low in self-esteem and, occasionally, socially immature. Whether this the cause of, or the result of, their learning difficulties need not concern us here, since the counsellor's aims are the same whatever the history of a child's problems might be. She knows the value of running a group for the children in which they can discuss with each other the problems they experience. In the safety of the group setting, they can begin to exchange ideas with each other as to the best ways of learning to overcome their problems.

Children with learning difficulties need help to see that they *can* achieve. Their motivation may be poor - indeed, some may have given up trying. Nevertheless, the group can give a child the feeling that he is not on his own, and that it is worth continuing to try. The counsellor also knows the value of using the opportunity to increase the children's feelings of confidence in a general sense. As with the counselling of other groups of children, she aims to encourage a free flow of ideas, and the expression of feelings - particularly, perhaps, the more negative feelings. All too often, these are bottled up, as the child struggles to please other people and to do what is expected of him.

Children with learning difficulties need to be helped to develop positive feelings about their abilities in other aspects of their lives. They may have practical or creative skills, or show good understanding of certain ideas and experiences. Reading and writing, though important, are not the only things that matter!

CHAPTER NINE

GROUP COUNSELLING AND SOCIAL SKILLS

As we have seen in the preceding chapter, group counselling can be used effectively with children with minor problems of social adjustment. It can also be used to help children with more serious problems of this nature: children sometimes described as emotionally or behaviourally disturbed (EBD). There is considerable scope here for helping children who are conspicuous through their disruptive, attention-seeking or excessively withdrawn behaviour to become accepted and acceptable members of their peer group. Counsellors will use different methods to achieve this goal, holding on to their counselling skills whilst adding others.

As we have seen in the previous chapter, each group which is run for children with particular difficulties (or special needs) presents its counsellor with its own challenge. As far as a group for children with major problems of social adjustment is concerned, the immediate challenge is that of encouraging the children to co-operate in establishing a group identity. Those who have experience of such children will be well aware that they have difficulty in controlling their own behaviour, sitting and listening to other people, co-operating in any group activity. In fact, the very attributes which the counsellor is hoping to help the children acquire are those which make it difficult to start the group and develop it! After a while, things tend to improve as the children become involved and begin to acquire more social skills, but in the beginning the counsellor(s) may have some difficulty in "holding" the group together in a cohesive manner, so that useful work with the children can take place.

Counsellors will have their own methods of starting the group and "holding" the participants. To some extent, it will depend on how the group comes about and in what setting it is taking place. It may be possible in some situations to include two or three ordinarily competent and sensible children of the same age to act as a stabilising factor. Counsellors may also decide that the group must have one or two basic rules such as no fighting or no interruptions whilst someone is talking. However the counsellor is also aware that the group loses its value if there are too many rules, since spontaneity and creativity tend to be lost.

Counsellors who run groups for children with major problems of social adjustment need skill and patience, linked with a confident expectation that change is possible. As in individual counselling, the counsellor's work needs to be based on the assumption that children have within themselves the potential for change. Improvement in the children is, however, unlikely to be rapid.

The aim of the group

Children with serious emotional and/or behavioural problems are very unlikely to be interested in joining in with group sessions. Unlike most socially competent and well-adjusted children, they do not enjoy the opportunity to communicate, discuss, reflect, share and consider their experiences. Some of the children find it almost impossible to put thoughts and feelings into words in a manner that allows for sensible consideration. Most will be hostile and suspicious of the adult's efforts to help them. Few, if any, will be enthusiastic participants.

Bearing in mind these difficulties, thecounsellor needs to have modest expectations of the children. Her goals must be, initially, at least, strictly limited. She needs to be honest with the children and tell them the purpose of the group - for example, that they have been selected for the group because adults are worried about their behaviour. The children should also be told that they will have the opportunity to say what *they* think (for example, about school rules or the behaviour of other people), but they will also be asked to do some listening.

The group counsellors (and there will probably need to be two of them, given the challenging nature of the children's behaviour) may decide to start the sessions by considering the need for change. Why is it not a good idea to behave rudely/swear at other people/disrupt lessons? Can the children see that it is better not to do these things— better for all concerned, including themselves? The counsellors will not be expecting positive or helpful comments from the children on these matters initially. The aim in the first instance is to introduce the idea of behavioural change. As the weeks go by, it should become increasingly possible for the children to co-operate,and this cooperation should eventually lead to an improvement in their attitude and behaviour.

A practical approach

Children with behavioural problems or problems of social adjustment are children who tend to "act out" their feelings rather than expressing them in a manner which allows for sensible discussion and negotiation. They also tend to be "locked into" their own view of things, and find it difficult to understand the feelings and viewpoint of other people. It is genuinely difficult for them, initially at least, to be part of a group which makes use of discussion and reflection as a means of promoting change. In her efforts to help the children, the counsellor may decide to incorporate certain activities into the group session(s). This could include the use of games, drama or role play, all of which can serve the purpose of promoting greater social awareness in the children. The choice of activity will depend on the children's age, and on the counsellor's feelings as to her own knowledge and competence.

Board games can be a useful means of demonstrating to children the need to listen, wait one's turn, co-operate with others, and to accept losing from time to time. They are particularly useful for younger children. Some counsellors, more ambitious and ideally appropriately trained, may feel able to make use of drama and role play, encouraging the children to act scenes which depict certain everyday experiences, particularly those of potential conflict. Examples might be the role play of a conversation between teacher and pupil about a playground incident or a lost homework book, or an argument between child and parent about staying out late in the evening. Situations should be chosen for their relevance to the children's experience and age-group. Initially the counsellor will need to make suggestions, but the children themselves will probably soon come up with their own ideas. (Those children who dislike this kind of activity should not, incidentally, be compelled to take part).

Role play, like the board games, is a means to an end not an end in itself. Once the scene has been played, the children who have taken part come "out of role" and, together with the children in the group who have not participated, discuss the implications of the scene. Did the children in the role play behave sensibly in their conversation with teachers or parents? If not, how might they have responded differently, or asked for what they wanted?

Whatever practical approaches are used by the counsellor to encourage children to develop greater social awareness and insight into their own behaviour, they are only useful insofar as whatever is learnt in the group can be applied outside it. It is here, of course, that the counsellor needs her counselling skills, as she helps the children to discuss the wider implications of the activities. At the same time, counsellors should be wary of making a *direct* link between what has been acted in the role play and a child's behaviour as the counsellor knows it to be. Rather, she aims to generate a discussion of the issues which the activity highlights, and to heighten children's awareness of social realities and of their own behaviour *indirectly*.

Problem-solving

The effective use of role play with groups of children needs particular expertise in the counsellor, and other methods of helping children to develop greater social awareness may be more generally useful. A "problem-solving" method, aimed at helping children to consider appropriate ways of tackling embarrassing or potentially explosive situations, can be very effective. In this method, the counsellor aims to introduce to the children the notion that there is always more than one way of acting - or reacting - in any given situation and that some ways are more useful than others.

There are different ways of encouraging the children to think about (solve) certain problems. The counsellor might, for example, decide to introduce a familiar topic - such as the need for punctuality. What happens when children are late for class? Why do teachers get cross? How do the other children feel? How can one learn to be punctual? Maybe it's impossible ....what do others think? Asking questions and encouraging the children to generate their own ideas, the counsellor hopes that unpunctual children will begin to realise why their behaviour is annoying to others - and, incidentally, unhelpful to themselves. The children are encouraged to consider how they might change, without directly having a finger pointed at them.

A counsellor might also decide to take an approach which is rather like a game. A number of cards can be prepared beforehand, each of which has a problem written on them, chosen to suit the client-group. The problems chosen need to be situations that are either potentially embarrassing , or associated with conflict - and ones which the children will recognise. One child draws a card, reads it, and the subject is open for discussion.

Examples might be:

"Another boy threatens you and asks you for money".

"You are angry because your best friend seems to prefer someone else".

"You borrowed your friend's bicycle without asking him. You left it unattended, and it was damaged by a passing car".

"Someone insults your sister".

Initially, some children may find it difficult to respond, and there may be some embarrassed laughter, or foolish or irrelevant comments, but over a period of time most of the children will be able to contribute to the discussion. No attempt need be made to "personalise" any of the issues, and children are not asked to say directly what they would do in any given circumstances. Instead, the method gives an opportunity to all to consider certain common dilemmas, listen to others as they make their contributions, and to consider various forms of action. The aim is, of course, to move children away from selfish, thoughtless or violent ways of dealing with problem situations, to ways which are based on negotiation with appropriate recourse to adult help when necessary.

Watching and learning

One of the important benefits which arise from working with groups rather than individuals is that group members have the opportunity to listen to, watch, and learn from other people. The learning takes place constantly, though not always predictably, and the counsellor needs to know how to create, or make use of, situations which are likely to be useful to the children.

Since the EBD child is so involved with himself and unable to see the viewpoint of other people, it can be extremely helpful if he hears other people talk about themselves and the difficulties *they* have experienced. It will probably come as a welcome relief - though he will not admit it - to a child to discover that he is not the only one to have certain difficulties in his relationships with others, or to feel angry and inadequate at times. It is also helpful if he can begin to hear how other people cope with difficult or embarassing situations. Eventually, he should gain sufficient confidence to bring out his own ideas.

Counsellors, listening carefully to the children, should know how to encourage (subtly) certain behaviour. The child who sits still and listens attentively, and the one who makes a point in a sensible fashion, may be rewarded with a friendly nod, whilst noisy and restless children need to be ignored as far as possible.

It is useful if the group contains a certain number of socially competent children who behave sensibly and make practical contributions to a discussion. However, the counsellor needs to be aware of the temptation to hold such children up as examples to others. EBD children are only too ready to feel inadequate, and to take refuge in their troubled or troublesome behaviour. The counsellor can aim to use the contributions of more socially competent children as a means of developing a conversation on a particular topic. At the same time, she listens carefully to less confident children, commenting favourably on any point which they make which indicates that they are thinking about themselves and their behaviour.

"Space" and the secure base

Children whose behaviour is disturbed are children with troubled feelings which they do not know how to express appropriately. The group should give each child an opportunity to put his feelings into words - including more negative feelings, such as anger, resentment, rivalry. This will initially be difficult for many of the children, most of whom are extremely defensive about their feelings and anxious above all to protect their self-esteem. It is so much easier to push or hit another child, rather than to admit that he has made you feel small or angry! It is also easier, in the short-term at least, to shout rudely at an adult who has scolded you, rather than apologise.

As the children become more confident in themselves and aware that (a) it is possible to admit to weakness and (b) everyone sometimes feels "bad", they will usually begin to put their thoughts and feelings into words more readily. The counsellor encourages this, since she knows that the child who understands and accepts his own negative feelings is the child who can begin to control them - or, at least, to avoid taking them out too violently on other people. She will therefore be conscious of the need to remind children of the normality of feeling unhappy, angry, jealous, foolish, whilst suggesting to them that it is not helpful to vent these feelings on others.

Working with her group, the counsellor offers the children space: to express an opinion, argue, disagree, remain silent. At the same time she provides a secure base, so that the children begin to see that it is not their feelings or their state of mind that has the potential to disrupt or destroy, but their behaviour. It is possible to communicate and be understood. It is also possible to learn to live with other people in a more socially acceptable manner.

CHAPTER TEN

MEETING THE PARENTS

With certain rare exceptions, children who see counsellors do so with their parents' knowledge. Agreement may be given directly by the parent, or it may be assumed in those situations (usually at school) where counselling is known to be available, and an accepted part of the facilities or curriculum offered to all children. But whatever the nature of the arrangement, it is incumbent on the counsellor to keep parents in mind, and to contact them if and when it seems to be necessary.

Sometimes parents are closely involved from the beginning. If they have referred the child themselves or given whole-hearted consent to the referral, it can be extremely helpful if they attend the initial interview with the child. This gives the counsellor the opportunity to ask the parents why they are worried about the child, and to encourage them to express their concern for him openly. Some parents find it difficult to discuss their child in front of him, but if they can be persuaded to do so it gives the counselling sessions a good start. The parents have recognised a problem and this encourages the child in turn to take the matter seriously. Equally as important, parental openness gives a clear message to the child that openness and honesty are both possible and desirable.

In some circumstances - perhaps in the majority of cases - counsellors do not see the parents of the children they are trying to help. Counsellors who work in some settings, particularly in schools, see a large number of children for a short period of time to help with relatively minor matters of adjustment, and parental involvement is neither necessary nor possible in all cases. However, when matters do not resolve themselves quickly, or when a particular child is behaving in a very worrying way, the counsellor will probably decide to contact the parents and arrange a meeting between them. She will, of course, discuss this with the child first and give a brief explanation of why she is taking this step - avoiding giving the impression that it is a punitive measure.

The purpose of the meeting

When a counsellor takes the initiative and contacts the parents of one of the children she is seeing, she should have some idea of what she hopes to gain from the interview. She may perhaps feel that certain information is needed, to allow her to understand and help the child more effectively. As we have seen, many children experience considerable distress as a result of family circumstances, and it is always helpful if the counsellor is aware of these circumstances. Children will sometimes tell the counsellor themselves of course, but a parental viewpoint is also useful.

Counsellors may also feel that a general discussion of the child and his past behaviour at home and at school would be useful. Parents can often contribute valuable information about this, which may indicate to the counsellor what steps, if any, others have already taken to help the child. This information helps the counsellor to decide what steps she herself might need to take. She may, for example, discover that the child and family have a social worker, or that they have been seen in the local psychological or psychiatric services. This information can be kept in hand should some additional help for the child be needed.

Sometimes children confide in their counsellors certain worries which their parents should know about, and the counsellor will feel that she should contact the parents on the child's behalf. Occasionally, this might be a serious matter, relating perhaps to an assault on the child. Less dramatically - though also important to a child - it may be a question of negotiating with the parents over issues of disagreement between parent and child. For example, a child whose parents are separated may wish to have more frequent contact with the absent parent. Or, a teenage girl may feel that she does not have the same freedom of movement as her peers. In these and similar situations the counsellor can sometimes help by putting the child's view to his parents, on his behalf. However, it can be a delicate task and the counsellor will not want to act impulsively. First of all, she will talk to the child himself about it. Has he approached his parents on the subject, and if so what was their response? She will also bear in mind possible parental opinions and prejudices. In some circumstances, where parents have deeply-rooted feelings of their own on a particular subject, any suggestions for change will probably not be acceptable.

When a child who has been seeing a counsellor for some time does not improve, or when there is a crisis (e.g. a violent incident) or a deterioration in his behaviour, the counsellor will feel the need to make a particular effort to meet the parents. Such meetings may be difficult, particularly if parents are angry at, say, a child's exclusion from school, but they can also be fruitful. They may even provide an opportunity for the counsellor to suggest that help from another agency might be best for the child, and to make a referral with parental permission (see following chapter).

The parental point of view

When inviting parents to attend an interview to discuss their child, counsellors need to remember that there may be circumstances which make it difficult for parents to accept. Many parents work long hours, and have no transport and little money. Some have younger children to care for, and no one with whom they can be left whilst parents attend an interview. Some parents do not speak English. A few are housebound through disability or illness. Even if there are no practical or physical reasons why a parent should not attend, he or she might find the prospect daunting. Parents whose lives are difficult do not relish the prospect of meeting someone who (they fear) will probably create further worries and anxieties for them. This may be reprehensible, but it is entirely understandable.

Counsellors need a sympathetic awareness of the parental viewpoint and of the genuine difficulties which many adults have in their lives. They will do their best to accommodate parental wishes in connection with the timing of an interview, and consider making a home visit if this is acceptable to the parents. However, they will be conscious of the need to avoid being too accommodating, in those situations where parents should be capable of making an effort on their own - and their child's - behalf.

Meeting the parents and talking about their child, counsellors need to be aware that the parents will almost certainly have a different view of the child from the one they have. Parents tend to identify quite strongly with their children and are often very defensive about them and their behaviour, and sensitive to possible criticism, even when none is intended. A counsellor needs therefore to avoid giving the impression of being an authority figure bent on criticising child or parent. She remembers to thank the parents for coming, and encourages them to give their own view of the child at an early stage, keeping her own comments to the minimum . She listens carefully to what is said, hoping to find clues that will help her to help the child. Choosing her moment carefully, she brings into the conversation those things which seem to her to be important, knowing that she must not labour the points, or overstate her case.

Each meeting has a purpose and the counsellor tries to hold on to this. At the same time, she keeps her counselling methods in mind, offering the parents time and space, and providing a secure base as they talk. She does not - should not - have too many hopes or expectations of a meeting with parents, nor should she try to be too ambitious. However, much can be done in a modest way through a friendly and sympathetic approach combined with a few suggestions to the parent as to what might be needed to help the child.

Those who counsel children cannot be counsellors - still less therapists - to parents, but they should know how to advise parents who admit to personal difficulties. In most parts of the country there are a range of services available to adults, offering help with marital problems, alcohol addiction, financial problems etc. Counsellors should know of these services in the area where they work, and pass on the information if it seems to be appropriate. It will of course be difficult to do this with parents whom one scarcely knows, and who have not directly asked for help for themselves. Many counsellors find it useful to have a series of leaflets advertising local agencies and services which might be helpful to parents, readily available and visible, perhaps pinned to a notice board in their rooms or just outside.

Understanding ambivalence

Those who counsel children soon become aware of the mixed feelings which they have for their parents, and the same is true of parents for their children. "I love him but I wish he wouldn't ...." is a very common emotion in people of all ages. However, people often feel badly about this, equating angry feelings with bad behaviour. Counsellors can often do much to help both children and parents come to terms with their mixed feelings, and to realise that anger with those whom they love is natural and not of itself a bad thing nor damaging to the recipient.

In the nature of things, parents hope that their children will be a credit to them. They invest a considerable amount of emotional energy in their offspring, and hope that life for them will be easier, and perhaps more successful, than it was for them (the parents). At the same time, there can be some uncertainty and even fear. "Is the child as clever as I'd like him to be?" "Might he turn out like his grandfather, who drinks too much?" "Will he outgrow his speech problem/bed-wetting/bad behaviour?" And, so often, the greatest anxiety of all: "Am I doing the right thing?"

These expectations and fears are very real, yet hard to admit to other people. Parents often prefer not to think about their children's problems, and to look for others to blame when things go wrong. Some have very unrealistically high expectations of their children; others have insufficient confidence in their potential for good development and sensible behaviour. In some cases there is a tendency to swing from one extreme to another, overprotecting the child in some circumstances and expecting him to behave like an adult in others.

Parents will also almost certainly have ambivalent feelings about the counsellor herself. On the one hand, there will be (probably) relief that someone is trying to help the child; on the other, the counsellor's involvement may be a source of guilt and anxiety to the parents - an unwelcome recognition that their child has a "problem" and needs help. Occasionally, there may be resentment and anger at what is seen as interference in family matters. The counsellor needs to understand these feelings and respect them, moving cautiously if she meets outright hostility. She knows that her meeting with the parents is worthwhile, and that she will often obtain certain information, or reach a certain understanding which allows her to help the child more effectively.

The "good enough" family

A counsellor's work, by its nature, brings her in contact with people with troubled lives. When the child is the client, it is so often the case that family circumstances are a contributory, even causative, factor. This is a fact of life which the experienced counsellor learns to accept.

As we have seen in earlier chapters, children can benefit immensely from an opportunity to discuss painful family matters in a confidential setting, and with help can come to terms with situations in their lives which cannot be changed. Nevertheless, there are times when counsellors feel confused and angered by parental behaviour and by the domestic circumstances of some of the children they see.

Some parents are, it must be recognised, not very good at meeting their children's developmental needs. A few are fundamentally neglectful or abusive of the child. This having been said, it must also be recognised that parents are the only adults who readily make a long-term commitment to a child, feeding and caring for him and putting up with the inconvenience of his behaviour and of the demands which he inevitably makes of them. Parents often do this in spite of serious personal difficulties, at times by sacrificing their own ambitions.

Donald Winnicott spoke of the "good enough" mother, using the expression to describe the reality of mothering in the vast majority of cases, and the concept can be extended to families. There are no ideal mothers, parents, families, merely individuals who are doing their best by their own lights to live their lives and bring up their children. Some manage better than others for many complex reasons, but very few are genuinely bad and beyond help.

The experienced counsellor knows that it is her job to help children co-operate with their families, except in rare and unusual circumstances when the family should be split and other people placed in a parental role. She hears complaints from children, but knows that they rarely want to be separated from their parents. Complaining is of itself beneficial, and the counsellor knows she should not confuse this with a request for action on the child's part. At the same time, she does occasionally have the painful duty to decide that "enough is enough" and, after a discussion with the child, to inform others that the home situation needs to be investigated.

Bridging the gap

From time to time counsellors become aware of the need to "bridge the gap"between parent and child, particularly during adolescence when some children become sufficiently desperate to consider leaving home, following a total breakdown in communication between themselves and their parents. The issues may seem relatively trivial, although they arouse intense feelings in those concerned. A child may want to stay out later in the evening than parents wish, have friends into the house, get a Saturday job and keep his own earnings, see an absent parent - and the parents may for one reason or another decide that the child's wishes are unreasonable. There may be additional difficulties which contribute to a breakdown in communication between parent(s) and child, such as lack of space and money, or the departure of one parent and arrival of a stepparent.

Counsellors can often see the danger signals, and try to act as negotiators. They are well aware that many of the domestic situations are far from ideal for the children they are trying to help, but they also know that the children need their families until they are sufficiently mature to stand on their own feet. They are also aware that their young clients are, like most adolescents, probably rude, untidy and generally difficult to live with! A joint interview (parent, child, counsellor) is often useful, if the counsellor feels able to meet with both parents and child at the same time. Topics which are a source of disagreement to both parties can be discussed and some solutions reached. It may be possible to draw up a contract, in which both parent and child agree to certain things on a "give and take" basis.

Counsellors may also find themselves "bridging the gap" between parent and teacher when a child has behaved badly at school. The parents' tendency to protect their child sometimes makes it difficult for them to accept the reality of what he has done. In some cases, this leads them to blame the school, or other children, or both. On the other hand, teachers some-times fail to see that a particular child is under stress, or finds it difficult to co-operate with others, be in the right place at the right time, sit still in the classroom. In these cases, where there is scope for misunderstanding and anger, counsellors can usefully meet with both parents and teachers for an open dis-cussion of the situation, in which the counsellor attempts to encourage co-operation between them .

At this point, we find ourselves moving away from the subject of personal counselling and towards a discussion of family therapy, or of mediation. These are different (though not to-tally unrelated) matters, involving rather different expertise and training. They will not necessarily be of interest to all of those who wish to counsel children.

I have considered elsewhere counselling in a "family sys-tems" framework (see Campion, *The Child in Context*, Chapter 13, Methuen, 1985). Interested counsellors will also find that there are many other books which can help them, if they wish to work with families, teachers, or other adults who come in contact with children.

CHAPTER ELEVEN

THE RESPONSIBILITIES OF THE COUNSELLOR

One of the difficulties that faces the trained and experienced counsellor is that others, untrained and inexperienced, will claim that they too "counsel" children. Such claims underestimate the counsellor's skills and they certainly undervalue her responsibilities. True, it is always possible for a sensible adult to lend an understanding ear and help a child in trouble, without training. However, the friendly ear and the helping hand are very different from the professional commitment which counsellors make to children with different problems of varying degrees of severity; as different, say, as are the skills of an adult who knows how to clean a wound and put on a dressing from those of a fully trained nurse.

Counsellors who work regularly with children with personal, social and/or behavioural problems such as those described in earlier chapters realise that their work entails not only skill, but considerable professional responsibility. One cannot undertake to invite a number of comparatively unknown children to relate personal experiences and confide their thoughts and feelings without accepting the fact that the invitation carries with it certain responsibilities, and occasional difficulties, for the adult listener. Nor can one claim to be a fully-fledged counsellor unless one is aware of the responsibilities of the work, and able to take account of them.

Training and support

The counsellor's first responsibility, both to herself and her clients, is to ensure that she is fully prepared for her work , and adequately supported by colleagues. It may not be possible to find a local training course which is designed specifically to meet the needs of child clients, but counsellors will benefit from one of the reputable, general personal counselling courses. It is then a question of adapting the skills acquired in training to meet the needs of children, whose problems and pre-occupations are, as we have seen, rather different from those of adults. It is also helpful, and possibly essential, for the counsellor to hold some recognised and relevant professional qualification, such as teaching, nursing or social work. Counselling as a career in its own right is still in its infancy, and these qualifications give the counsellor credibility, and protection in her work.

Counsellors will also need to attend additional courses, which are relevant to the needs of their own client group. Those who counsel children should be informed as to the recognised procedures for dealing with sexual abuse, and also of the effects of drug abuse. Those who work in particular institutions such as schools or hospitals need to ensure that they are familiar with the structure of these institutions, and the roles of those who work in them if they do not already have this knowledge. Counsellors of sick or disabled children need to learn something of their various medical conditions and of the treatments which they are likely to receive.

Most counsellors will find it helpful to attend courses which teach skills that are related to counselling. Courses on groupwork and on role play are particularly useful, although they may not be widely available. It is also helpful if the counsellor can develop her technique at interviewing parents, and perhaps in working with families. However, much will depend on what is available locally, as well as on the counsellor's own personal needs and inclinations. Above all, counsellors need to recognise that counselling is not an exercise involving the rigid application of particular techniques, but a dynamic and flexible process in which the counsellor is continually learning and applying new skills and understanding. The need for self-evaluation and self-development never ceases, and good counsellors are continually aware of the need to extend their skills in whatever manner seems feasible.

Counsellors, even when they are experienced, should take the opportunity from time to time to consult with other people, particularly when they are faced with a difficult or unusual case. They also need time to discuss their work more generally with an experienced colleague. Counselling can be stressful, and counsellors should ensure that they have a regular link with an appropriate agency, such as the school psychological service or child guidance clinic, to help them work as efficiently as possible.

Commitment to the client

Counselling involves a commitment to the client that is both practical and personal. From a practical point of view, the counsellor tries to ensure that she works in an organised manner, with certain goals in mind for her clients. Although each case is different and it is hard to generalise, she will probably aim to see a client for about four or five sessions at weekly intervals, and then to reconsider her position. She is hoping to see some signs of improvement in the child after this time, such as greater confidence, better school attendance, more sensible behaviour. If there is improvement, she may decide to continue for another two or three sessions, perhaps at more widely spaced intervals before finishing with the child. If there is no improvement, she may want to re-think (see below).

During the period of time in which she is working with a particular child, the counsellor knows that it is important to keep meticulously to the arrangements agreed between them, as to time and place of the sessions. Even if the child fails to respect this, the counsellor must not. If she cannot be present at a particular session for unavoidable reasons, she should make sure that the child knows about this and is offered an apology and a substitute time.

The counsellor needs to indicate to a child that the sessions will not continue indefinitely. It may be hard to know if a child is pleased or sorry about this. For some children the sessions are welcome, but for others they remain to some extent associated with ideas of discipline. However, in all cases the counsellor needs to indicate that the sessions have a purpose and that they will end when things have improved. She may feel that some children need to be told at the end of the sessions that they may come back again to see her if they wish. However, in my experience, relatively few children take up the suggestion. Having benefited from the sessions, most move on and take their place alongside their peers.

Sometimes children do not improve in spite of the counsellor's efforts, and occasionally a child suffers a crisis in his life while he is seeing the counsellor. Circumstances such as these suggest that there may be a need for a change of direction, and the counsellor should take time to discuss the case with an experienced colleague. Her commitment to the client remains, but the intervention may need to be changed. She should contact the child's parents for a discussion of the child's needs and the facilities available to help him, and may occasionally need to contact other agencies.

But the counsellor's commitment to her client cannot be considered solely in terms of practicalities. The relationship between counsellor and child is a very personal one and, like any other personal relationship, subject to certain emotional factors. During the time she is seeing the child, the counsellor commits herself to him and his problems, and devotes her energies to helping him overcome whatever difficulties he is experiencing. He is important to her, and she hopes that he will make progress until he no longer needs her help. On the other hand, she must accept that there are limits to what she is able to achieve for certain children, and that sometimes she will fail. In the nature of the work, some of her young clients will have problems which are too complex for her to be able to tackle alone.

Commitment to a client over a period of time can create certain difficulties for both counsellor and client. There is a slight possibility that a counsellor will begin to feel too close an involvement with certain children, and become unable to see weaknesses which other people see. Such close identification with a child and his particular difficulties can prevent a counsellor from helping a child to develop the personal strengths he needs, if he is to make his way in the world and keep out of trouble.

Accepting the limitations

Counselling is a skill which is designed to help people help themselves, by encouraging them to think about their behaviour, their circumstances and their relationships with other people. It is accepted that there is a problem in the life of the client which needs to be addressed. It is also assumed that people have within themselves the potential to change their behaviour, attitudes and feelings and that the counsellor will be able to help them in this. With rare exceptions, the counsellors' goals are strictly limited. Counsellors are not trained to provide "in-depth" work with highly disturbed clients, nor does their brief permit them to take certain radical steps on a child's behalf (e.g. making a recommendation for special schooling). If they feel that their young client needs this kind of provision, they must seek the help of other agencies. Indeed, part of the counsellor' s skill lies in knowing when one can do no more for a child and how to elicit the help of other people who have the necessary skills and resources.

Counsellors need to be able to accept their own limitations to help certain children, and they also need to be wary of giving their clients the impression that they have greater powers than they do. The adult client is well aware that counsellors cannot " fix things" for him, but children may have an unrealistic view of the counsellor's powers. It is therefore important that the counsellor does not give a child the impression that she can, for example, change the rules of the school he attends or bring together his separated parents. This may seem obvious to the adult, but it may well not be to the child.

Confidentiality

Counsellors take for granted the need to respect the privacy of their clients, and to keep secret the things they are told during counselling sessions, except in certain unusual circumstances. Some counsellors like to tell their clients at the outset that the sessions are confidential, but there are good reasons for not doing this. There really is no need to discuss confidentiality with child clients, since the children themselves will probably not think about it and the counsellor risks promising something unnecessarily which she may not be able to fulfil.

Most of what is said to a counsellor is not of a nature that makes her think she should pass the information to other people . Counsellors hear children's complaints, and worries about themselves and their relationships with other people, and know how valuable it is for the child to have her attention. Rarely is it necessary to communicate what is said in a session to others.

Nevertheless, there are occasions when a counsellor needs to pass on certain information. Like any other adult, she has a duty to report child abuse to the appropriate authorities (police or the social services department), although she will explain to the child himself first of all why she must take this step. She may also decide that it is necessary to tell others when she is worried about a particular child, even if she does not suspect abuse. In these cases, she may well not report in detail what the child has told her, but rather communicate her worries about him in a general manner, perhaps to the local child psychological or psychiatric services.

From time to time, counsellors may hear of certain rather dubious matters which may not involve the the child himself, but those known to him. These are not necessarily issues which put a child "at risk", but activities or incidents which are illegal or immoral, such as shop-lifting, vandalism, and certain sexual activities. It is impossible to make rules about what should or should not be divulged, and counsellors will have to make their own decisions based on what seems to be reasonable in each case.

Responsibility to parents

A counsellor realises that she has a responsibility to a child's parents and will always, except in the briefest of interventions (e.g. one or two sessions with a child in school concerning a minor incident which is not repeated) contact them and inform them that she is seeing their child. She may well decide to offer an open invitation to a child's parents to meet her at a mutually convenient time. Alternatively, she may fix a date and send them an appointment.

As we have seen in preceding chapters, contact with parents is not always straightforward. Although most parents have their children's best interests at heart, many have considerable personal difficulties and responsibilities which make it hard for them to attend interviews. Many are (in my experience) quite content for the counselling to proceed without them, and some will express gratitude for the help offered to their child.

Although contact with parents may not be easy, counsellors should persist. A telephone call in the evening for a brief chat may be useful, or a short letter making a few comments about the child's progress. Of course, if a child continues to give cause for concern over a period of time, it will be necessary to put some pressure on a parent to attend so that alternative means of helping a child are discussed.

Counsellors know that they must respect parental rights and ensure that they do not say or do anything that risks "splitting" parent and child. To side with a child against his parent is always risky, even if the subject under discussion is not important. Rather, the counsellor's goal is to see both sides of a situation and to help the child on this basis if possible. If this is not possible and parental behaviour is intolerable from the child's point of view, the counsellor will need to seek help which may lead in some circumstances to the child being removed from his family.

Contact with other professionals

Each counsellor will have her own working arrangements, but none should work in complete isolation. In some cases, there will be a requirement for the counsellor to be supervised in her work by a senior colleague; in others, she may be left very much to her own devices. In this case, she should try to arrange for regular contact with others who are involved in the welfare, education and development of children (see below).

Regular contact with experienced colleagues gives the counsellor the opportunity to discuss difficult or unusual cases, or to seek advice when a particular child does not seem to be improving. It should also help her to avoid the error of becoming too closely involved with a particular child. Quite often, the opportunity to discuss a case helps the counsellor clarify her own ideas, so that she is able to introduce a slightly different method of working with a child, to his advantage. It can also help the counsellor to decide whether or not she is able to continue with a particular case, and to whom she should refer it if necessary.

Contact with others also helps the counsellor develop the range of her own skills and understanding. Sometimes it is possible to undertake groupwork with another counsellor, and both can learn from each other. As we have seen, counselling is a very personal skill, and counsellors can usually benefit from new ideas and approaches, gleaned from others with similar responsibilities.

Contact with others also gives the counsellor emotional support and encouragement. Counselling is an immensely rewarding job, but it is also stressful and in some respects lonely. It is a great relief to be able to share the burden, and the pleasures, with other people who have similar responsibilities.

The professional network

Each local authority has a number of agencies concerned with the welfare, protection and development of children, although the names by which these agencies are known vary from area to area. The psychological services for children (or school psychological services) are probably the first port of call for the counsellor who needs general support and advice on certain children. They consist of a group of educational psychologists who themselves usually counsel certain children, and perhaps also specialist teachers or social workers with counselling skills. Child psychotherapists and child psychiatrists may also work as part of the team, or in close liaison with it.

Counsellors who work in schools have automatic access to the educational psychologists in the area. Others should be able to make contact with the local child guidance clinics if it is not possible for them to make use of the school psychological service. All should know how to contact the local social services department. However, it is worth remembering that all the services are hard pressed, and that the number of children who need help invariably outstrips the number of people available to offer it. Counsellors who would seek their help or advice may need to persist, unless their case must have urgent attention. In some parts of the country, for example, social workers are only able to deal with cases of sexual or physical abuse and there is no time for other work.

All counsellors will from time to time come in contact with a child whom it is extremely difficult to help. These are children whose behaviour continues to give cause for concern in spite of the counsellor's help, and those who live in circumstances which are highly damaging and need to be investigated by the appropriate agencies. Such cases need careful handling and should be discussed with experienced colleagues. Other forms of help may be needed, such as psychotherapy, family therapy, special schooling - or, in exceptional cases, reception into Care.

CHAPTER TWELVE

A QUESTION OF CONFIDENCE

There has always been a need for child counsellors, although their work has never been given the recognition it deserves. Today, the need is greater than it has ever been. An increase in the number of cases of child abuse and neglect is reported. In addition, teachers, social workers and those who work in the field of child psychology and psychiatry are conscious of the very large number of children who are troubled or troublesome, delinquent, regularly out of school, glue-sniffing or drug-taking. An increase in the amount of breakdown in family life means that many children suffer distress or depression as they struggle to adapt themselves to new domestic circumstances.

I have tried to demonstrate that counselling is a valuable means of bringing about behavioural change, as well as a means of helping troubled children. In doing so, I hope I have not given the impression that it is an "easy option", or that it should be seen as the only means of helping a child behave acceptably. Clearly, children must learn to obey rules and to accept punishment in certain circumstances. Equally, adults need to be confident in setting certain limitations on children's behaviour. Counsellors know this, and are aware of the need to work within these guidelines, without undermining the authority of others, except in very rare and unusual circumstances.

I have also tried to speak of children and their problems in rather general terms, while at the same time recognising that each child's situation is unique, and must be considered as such by the counsellor concerned. In many cases, the position is complex - much more complex than I have indicated in my description of certain children in the preceding pages. In an attempt to focus mainly on children and their counsellors, I have inevitably omitted certain details and simplified certain issues. For example, relatively little attention is paid to parental behaviour and attitudes towards the children, and even less to that of their teachers. This is not because they are unimportant; on the contrary, they matter very much. However, I was anxious not to stray too far away from the central theme and into a wider consideration of what can be done to help vulnerable children in schools and in the community, and through the school psychological services and child guidance clinics.

I am conscious too, of having neglected certain topics which some might regards as important, in particular the thorny subject of children's sexuality and the issue of racial and cultural differences. Both these subjects are complex and arouse strong feelings in many adults. As far as children's sexuality is concerned, I do not on the whole feel that it is anything like as important to the children themselves as more ordinary problems such as getting on with family and friends, feeling reasonably good about oneself, and keeping out of trouble. However, I am aware that some adults attach great importance to such subjects as early sexual relationships, sexual identity/orientation, contraception, sexually-transmitted diseases etc. I am also aware that there are many differing viewpoints on the subject! From a practical point of view, I feel sure that a sensible and well-trained counsellor can take these things in her stride, tackling each child's problem as it comes her way.

As far as racial and cultural issues are concerned, the picture is even more complicated, particularly in certain parts of the country. Is it possible, one wonders, for an English (Welsh, Scots, Irish) counsellor to counsel, say, a Muslim girl who tells her at school that she is experiencing certain difficulties in her relationship with her parents, or an Afro-Caribbean child who feels that he is being subjected to racial discrimination? Some would say no. But then again, why not?

In today's society, where there are so many different adult attitudes and so many changes, and where a number of people suffer from considerable hardship and the outlook seems very uncertain, it needs courage to give a confident message for the future to tomorrow's adults. Those who counsel children must try, sticking to those things that are of fundamental importance to their clients: family and friends, self-esteem, feeling able to cope with the demands of everyday life. Counsellors need a balanced and realistic view of the world and a relatively mature understanding of what is - and is not - appropriate and acceptable, They also need confidence in their own judgement, particularly in those difficult cases when it seems that the help of other people or other agencies might be needed.

But above all counsellors need confidence in the children themselves, and in their potential for good development. Time and again this proves to be justified, as certain children demonstrate that they are able to make an effort on their own behalf, or come to terms with difficult or unhappy circumstances. Much can be achieved, with patience, and with understanding.

SOME SUGGESTED READING

BOWLBY, J. (1988) *A Secure Base*. London, Routledge.

CROSS, J. and GODDARD,S. (1988) Social skills training in the ordinary school setting, *Educational Psychology in Practice*, Vol.4, No.1. Longman.

GLASER, D. and FROSH, S. (1988) *Child Sexual Abuse*. London: Macmillan Educational Ltd.

KELLMER-PRINGLE, M. (1975) *The Needs of Children*. London: Hutchinson.

KREMENTZ. J. (1983) *How It Feels When a Parent Dies*. London: Gollancz.

MEARNS, D. and THORNE, B. (1988) *Person-Centred Counselling in Action*. Series ed. Windy Dryden. Sage Publications.

MURGATROYD, S. (1980) *Helping the Troubled Child* .London: Harper and Row.

NOONAN, E. (1983) *Counselling Young People*. London: Methuen.

WALCZAK, Y. and BURNS, S. (1984) *Divorce: The Child's Point of View*. London: Harper and Row.

WINNICOTT, D.W. (1965) *The Family and Individual Development*. London: Tavistock.

WINNICOTT, D.W. (1971) *Playing and Reality*. London: Tavistock.

Useful address: British Association for Counselling, 37a Sheep Street, Rugby, Warwickshire, CV21 3BX.